"Solid insightful answers to difficult and intriguing questions that only Geisler could do. A must-read."

—**Josh D. McDowell**, Author/speaker,
  Campus Crusade for Christ

"Norm Geisler has made a marked impact in the study of apologetics, contending for the remarkable gift of faith with which God has blessed His creation. Tackling one of the most misunderstood realities—evil in the world—Norm has shed the light of God's Word in a clear and unmistakable way in helping the human mind to rejoice in the vastness of God's love that will ultimately overcome evil victoriously. Your heart will be greatly enlightened and comforted as you read *If God, Why Evil?*"

—**Franklin Graham**, President & CEO,
  Billy Graham Evangelistic Association, Samaritan's Purse

"This small book by Norman Geisler concisely answers the big questions on the problem of evil. It is a "crash course" that dispels confusion and brings clarity to this much-debated topic. Highly recommended!"

—**Dr. Ron Rhodes**, President,
  Reasoning from the Scriptures Ministries

"For more than five decades, Norm Geisler has been an incredible blessing to the church, addressing and treating virtually every major issue in the philosophy of religion. In this volume, he wades into one of his favorite subjects—the problem of evil. He faces squarely the major objections from a variety of angles and provides a wide range of concise responses that are both profound and satisfying. Readers should encounter countless gems that make this volume a real treasure. I recommend it highly."

—**Gary R. Habermas**, Distinguished Research Professor,
  Liberty University & Theological Seminary

"No one deals as effectively with the philosophical problem of evil as does Norm Geisler. *If God, Why Evil?* is scholarship made readable for every thinking Christian. As usual, Geisler is succinct, profound, and fun all at the same moment."

—**Paige Patterson**, Southwestern Baptist
Theological Seminary

"Norm Geisler has done exactly what he has promised—written a clear, concise, comprehensive, corrrect, and comforting volume on the question of evil. This issue, and all related concerns, are faced by every Christian in their own mind and in their witness to others. That's why this book is an absolute must-read!'

—**Dr. R. Philip Roberts**, President,
Midwestern Baptist Theological Seminary

A New Way to Think About the Question

If God, Why Evil?

NORMAN L. GEISLER

BETHANY HOUSE PUBLISHERS

Minneapolis, Minnesota

Published by Bethany House Publishers
11400 Hampshire Avenue South
Bloomington, Minnesota 55438

Bethany House Publishers is a division of
Baker Publishing Group, Grand Rapids, Michigan.

Printed in the United States of America

In keeping with biblical principles of creation stewardship, Baker Publishing Group advocates the responsible use of our natural resources. As a member of the Green Press Initiative, our company uses recycled paper when possible. The text paper of this book is comprised of 30% post-consumer waste.

green press INITIATIVE

Library of Congress Cataloging-in-Publication Data

Geisler, Norman L.
    If God, why evil? : a new way to think about the question / Norman L. Geisler.
        p. cm.
    Includes bibliographical references.
    ISBN 978-0-7642-0812-6 (pbk. : alk. paper) 1. Theodicy. I. Title.
    BT160.G35   2011
    231'.8—dc22

2010038736

About the Author

DR. NORMAN L. GEISLER has taught at the university and graduate levels for more than fifty years and has spoken and debated all over the world. He holds an MA from Wheaton College and a PhD in philosophy from Loyola University, and is presently Provost and Distinguished Professor of Apologetics at Veritas Evangelical Seminary (*www.VeritasSeminary.com*) in Murrieta, California. He is the author or coauthor of more than 70 books.

A SELECTION OF BOOKS
BY NORMAN L. GEISLER

Chosen But Free, rev. ed. (Bethany House, 2010)

Christian Ethics, rev. ed. (Baker, 2010)

The Apologetics of Jesus (Baker, 2009)

Conversational Evangelism (Harvest House, 2009)

Making Sense of Bible Difficulties (Baker, 2009)

The Big Book of Bible Difficulties (Baker, 2008)

Conviction Without Compromise (Harvest House, 2008)

When Skeptics Ask (Baker, 1990, 2008)

Creation in the Courts (Crossway, 2007)

A Popular Survey of the New Testament (Baker, 2007)

A Popular Survey of the Old Testament (Baker, 1977, 2007)

Why I Am a Christian, rev. ed. (Baker, 2001, 2006)

Correcting the Cults (Baker, 2005)

Systematic Theology Vols. 1–4 (Bethany House, 2002–2005)

I Don't Have Enough Faith to Be an Atheist (Crossway, 2004)

Who Made God? And An Answer to 100 Other Tough Questions (Zondervan, 2003)

Answering Islam, rev. ed. (Baker, 2002)

Unshakable Foundations (Bethany House, 2001)

The Battle for God (Kregel, 2001)

Baker Encyclopedia of Christian Apologetics (Baker, 1999)

Legislating Morality (Bethany House, 1998)

Creating God in the Image of Man? (Bethany House, 1997)

When Cultists Ask (Victor, 1997)

Love Is Always Right (Thomas Nelson, 1996)

Roman Catholics and Evangelicals (Baker, 1995)

In Defense of the Resurrection, rev. ed. (Witness, Inc., 1993)

When Critics Ask (Victor, 1992)

Miracles and the Modern Mind (Baker, 1992)

Matters of Life and Death (Baker, 1991)

Thomas Aquinas: An Evangelical Appraisal (Wipf & Stock, 1991)

The Life and Death Debate (Greenwood, 1990)

Gambling: A Bad Bet (Revell, 1990)

Come Let Us Reason (Baker, 1990)

Apologetics in the New Age (Baker, 1990)

Introduction to Philosophy (Baker, 1987, 1990)

The Battle for the Resurrection (Thomas Nelson, 1989)

The Infiltration of the New Age (Tyndale, 1989)

Knowing the Truth About Creation (Servant, 1989)

Worlds Apart (Baker, 1989)

Christian Apologetics (Baker, 1988)

Signs and Wonders (Tyndale, 1988)

Philosophy of Religion (Wipf & Stock, 1988)

Origin Science (Baker, 1987)

The Reincarnation Sensation (Tyndale, 1986)

A General Introduction to the Bible, rev. ed. (Moody, 1986)

False Gods of Our Time (Harvest House, 1985)

To Drink or Not to Drink (Quest, 1984)

Explaining Hermeneutics (ICBI, 1983)

Is Man the Measure? (Wipf & Stock, 1983)

Miracles and Modern Thought (Zondervan, 1982)

What Augustine Says (Baker, 1982)

The Creator in the Courtroom: Scopes II (Baker, 1982)

Decide for Yourself (Zondervan, 1982)

Biblical Errancy (Zondervan, 1981)

Options in Contemporary Christian Ethics (Baker, 1981)

Inerrancy (Zondervan, 1980)

To Understand the Bible, Look for Jesus (Baker, 1979)

From God to Us (Moody, 1974)

Contents

Introduction

In my fifty years of studying difficult questions, none is asked more often than "If God exists, then why is there so much evil in the world?" This is near the top of virtually all lists of the most asked questions about the Christian faith. Despite this, I know of no short, simple, readable, and comprehensive book on the topic. *If God, Why Evil?* attempts to fill this gap.

Judging by the popularity of books like *The Shack* (see appendix 3), people are hungering for a truly comforting answer when faced with suffering, tragedy, and death. I know this from personal experience. I have lost my father, my mother, my sister, and (hardest of all) my daughter. My heart goes out to anyone who has experienced any of these evils. They are real, and they really hurt.

At the same time our heart needs comfort, our head needs answers. If there is an all-good and all-powerful God, then why does He not put a stop to all of these tragedies? Better yet, if He knew the sum total of human misery that has occurred would occur, then why did He create this world to begin with?

From a purely apologetic perspective, more skepticism, agnosticism, and atheism have sprung from an inability to answer various aspects of the problem of evil than from any other single issue. What is more, when doubt begins in this area, it moves quickly to other areas. The problem of evil is a kingpin factor.

Admittedly, many books have been written on various aspects of this problem. What's different about this book? First, this work attempts to be *clear* about the various dilemmas and the proposed solutions. The problem is clearly stated first and then an answer is offered in basic terms.

Second, this book is *concise*. The problems and responses are put in succinct logical form so that one can see plainly what is being said. Elaboration is kept to a minimum so that one does not get lost in the forest for the trees.

Third, this book is *comprehensive*. Just a glance at the chapters reveals this, for the book treats evil's nature, origin, persistence, purpose, and avoidability. It discusses evil's metaphysical, moral, and physical problems. In addition, it speaks about why God does not perform more miracles to avert evil and why He, according to the Bible, allows some people to suffer forever (in hell).

Fourth, this work attempts to be *correct*. We are not engaging in mere intellectual exercises; we are searching for truth. Since we believe that God is the source of all truth and that the Bible is an authoritative revelation from Him, we seek to be biblical.

Finally, this book seeks to be *comforting*. We are not interested only in intellectual solutions but in practical ones as well. Hence real-life situations are scattered throughout the book, showing the personal value of the solutions to evil.

It is my fervent hope and prayer that you will gain as much from reading *If God, Why Evil?* as I have after a half century of pondering these matters.

Chapter 4

Three Views on Evil

I vividly remember my first debate with an atheist, at Lake County Community College, north of Chicago. He claimed the untold evil in the world demonstrates that there cannot possibly be a God. When I asked by what moral standard he was making this judgment, he immediately realized he was on the horns of a dilemma. If he admitted there is an ultimate moral law by which he knew the world to be evil, then this would lead to an ultimate Moral Lawgiver. If he denied an objective moral law, then this would seem to wipe away any solid grounds for his complaint against God.

His answer was frank but shocking: "I don't have any ultimate moral law by which I am making my judgment that this world is evil. My conclusion is simply based on my own benign moral feeling." Of course, had I said my basis for believing in God was not based on any objective evidence—only my own benign moral feeling—I would have been laughed off the platform.

Everyone experiences evil. It comes in many forms: pain, suffering, disease, disaster, death. Everyone seeks an answer to the questions: Is there any purpose to pain? Why did my loved one die? Why was our town bashed by the hurricane? Why did lightning strike our home? Why did the tornado rage through our neighborhood? Why do so many die of drought and starvation? A person would have to be totally insensitive not to wonder about the problem of evil.

Three basic answers to the overall problem have been offered.

> Pantheism *affirms God and denies evil.*
> Atheism *affirms evil and denies God.*
> Theism *affirms both God and evil.*

In general, pantheists believe God exists but deny the existence of evil. They believe God is good, God is All, and hence there is no evil. Mary Baker Eddy, founder of Christian Science, held this view, maintaining that "evil is an error of [the] moral mind."

Most people, however, find it difficult to accept this answer. The old limerick summarizes their conundrum well:

> There was a Faith Healer of deal
> Who said "Although pain isn't real,
> If I sit upon a pin,
> And it punctures my skin,
> I dislike what I fancy I feel!"

In short, if evil is not real, then why does it hurt so badly? If pain, suffering, and death are not real, then how do we explain where the illusion came from? And why does everyone have it? Further, why is the illusion so persistent? Why can't we make it go away? When we wonder whether we are dreaming or awake, we can pinch ourselves. We know we have been dreaming because we wake up. But we don't wake up from suffering, which always surrounds us and often invades us. We can tell an illusion because there is always a backdrop of reality by which we know it is an illusion. But evil is part of the backdrop of life itself. How then can it be illusory?

The atheist's solution to evil is just the opposite. Atheists admit that evil is real, but do not believe God is. Sigmund Freud claimed that God is an illusion because belief in God is based on wish fulfillment. He said that while it would be nice if there were a God, it also would be nice if there were a pot of gold at the end of the rainbow.

However, we can only know something is evil (not good) if we know what is good.

We can't know something is *injust* unless we know what is just. But if there is a moral law demanding that we ought always to be just, this leads us right back to a Moral Lawgiver. C. S. Lewis said, "[When I was an atheist] my argument against God was that the universe seemed so cruel and unjust. But how had I got this idea of just and unjust? A man does not call a line crooked unless he has some idea of a straight line" (*Mere Christianity*, 45).

Further, Freud confused a wish and a need. That we wish something to exist does not mean it does. But it is reasonable to believe that if we truly need something, then it does exist. Scientist and head of the human genome project, Francis Collins, puts it this way:

> Why would such a universal and uniquely human hunger [for God] exist, if it were not connected to some opportunity for fulfillment? Creatures are not born with desires unless satisfaction for those desires exists. A baby feels hunger: well, there is such a thing as food. A duckling wants to swim: well, there is such a thing as water. (*The Language of God*, 38)

Even atheists have demonstrated a need for God. Jean-Paul Sartre said, "I needed God. . . . I reached out for religion, I longed for it, it was the remedy. Had it been denied me, I would have invented it myself" (*Words*, 102, 197). Albert Camus added, "Nothing can discourage the appetite for divinity in the heart of man" (*The Rebel*, 147). As the scientist and mathematician Blaise Pascal noted, there is a God-sized vacuum in every heart that can be filled only by the One who made it:

> What else does this craving proclaim . . . but that there was once in man a true state of happiness, of which all that now remains is the empty print and trace? This he tries in vain to fill with everything around him . . . though none can help, since this infinite abyss can be filled only with an infinite and immutable object, in other words by God himself. (*Pensees*, #148)

This leaves us with the remaining alternative that both God and evil are real. But this nonetheless is a real problem—at least for the Christian view of God. The God of the Bible is all-knowing, and He foresaw that evil would occur in His world. He also is all-good, and He desires to do away with evil. In addition, He is all-powerful and could accomplish this. Why then does evil exist? Are not good and evil opposites? How can the existence of evil be reconciled with the existence of an all-good, all-powerful God?

Rabbi Harold Kushner offered a simple solution to this dilemma in his bestseller *When Bad Things Happen to Good People*: God is neither all-good nor all-powerful.

> If we can bring ourselves to acknowledge that there are some things God does not control, many good things become possible . . . (45). Are you capable of forgiving God even when you have found out that He is not perfect? (148)

However, there are several serious issues with this view of God. First, as C. S. Lewis observed, how can we know something is not perfect unless we know what is perfect? So if there were a *not*-perfect being that permitted or inflicted evil on this world, then such a being would not be God but a devil. The imperfect implies a perfect standard (God) by which we measure the not perfect. Kushner's imperfect god implies that there is a perfect God beyond this imperfect world.

Second, Kushner's god is not all-powerful, being finite and limited in power. However, everything that is limited is limited by something else, which eventually leads us to an Unlimited Limiter of every limited being. Thus Kushner's god is a violation of the fundamental law of causality, i.e., that every limited being has a cause.

A parable will illustrate this point. An atheist and a theist went for a walk in the woods and came upon a glass ball about eight feet in diameter. They both wondered where it came from and agreed that someone or something must have put it there. The theist then asked, "If the ball were sixteen feet in diameter, would it still need a cause?"

"Of course," replied the atheist. "If little spheres need causes, then so do larger ones."

"Ah, so," said the theist, "then what if it were eight thousand miles in diameter—would it still need a cause?"

The atheist paused and said, "Yes, if little spheres need causes and larger ones do too, then a really big one would also need a cause."

Then the theist said, "What if we make the ball as big as the whole universe: would it still need a cause?"

"Of course not," snapped the atheist. "The universe is just there!"

And there is the problem, namely, that making the ball bigger does not eliminate the need for a cause—it demands an even greater Cause. So a finite (limited) god needs a cause. Since every *finite* being needs a cause, the Cause of all finite beings (God) does not need a cause: He is the Uncaused Cause and Unlimited Limiter of all limited things. Kushner's god does not solve the problem but calls for another, more ultimate answer.

THE PROBLEM STILL REMAINS

The Christian (theist) claims that only an infinitely good and infinitely powerful God can solve the problem of evil (see chapter 4). But how? Again, are not absolute good and evil incompatible? And could not an all-good and all-powerful God eliminate evil?

Chapter 2

The Nature of Evil

The reality of evil has led some great minds to conclude that evil must be co-eternal with good. Augustine was one such mind. As a young man he was attracted to the Manichaean religion because it seemed to have an answer to this perplexing problem: If evil is real, and if it is opposed to good, then both good and evil must have existed forever. How he worked his way out of this thinking and ultimately became a Christian is a fascinating story, told in his *Confessions*. The result was a profound understanding of the nature of good and evil, which he shared in his anti-Manichaean writings (and of which we are the beneficiaries).

STATEMENT OF THE PROBLEM OF THE NATURE OF EVIL

Before we can answer where evil came from, we need to ask what evil is. Very simply, the problem of the nature of evil initially can be put this way:

1. God created all things.

2. Evil is something.
3. Therefore, God created evil.

The Christian (theist) cannot deny the first premise. The Bible declares that God created all things. "In the beginning God created the heavens and the earth" (Genesis 1:1); "All things were made through Him, and without Him nothing was made that was made" (John 1:3 NKJV); "By him all things were created: things in heaven and on earth, visible and invisible" (Colossians 1:16); the saints in heaven sing to God, "You created all things, and by your will they existed and were created" (Revelation 4:11 ESV).

Likewise, it would appear a biblical Christian cannot deny that evil is something real. The Bible declares the reality of sin and death: "Through one man sin entered the world, and death through sin, and thus death spread to all men, because all sinned" (Romans 5:12 NKJV); "the wages of sin is death" (6:23). To deny evil's reality is to deny the Bible and human experience. Paul declared, "What a wretched man I am! Who will rescue me from this body of death?" (7:24); "I know that nothing good lives in me" (7:18).

But if God created all things (first premise), and if evil is something (second premise), then must God have created evil (third premise)? The Bible makes it clear that God created only *good* things. After almost every day of creation God said, "It is good." Looking back on all His creation, "It was very good" (Genesis 1:31). Paul adds, "Everything God created is good" (1 Timothy 4:4); indeed, no food "is unclean in itself" (Romans 14:14). Accordingly, young Augustine and every thinking Christian since is faced with this: If everything God made was good, then how can evil be real? Or, if evil is real, then how can God not have created it?

RESPONSE TO THE PROBLEM OF THE NATURE OF EVIL

The reply is found in what is meant by a "thing" (substance). Certainly, a Christian must admit that God did create every "thing" or substance (a thing in itself). But we need not agree that there are evil "things." How then can evil be real but not a thing? Augustine found a satisfying, enduring answer: *Evil is a real lack, privation, or corruption of a good thing.* That is, evil does not exist in itself: evil exists only in a thing or substance— and all things God made are good. In short, there has to be some good thing in order for evil to exist in it as a lack, corruption, or privation of it. So to restate the argument against God from the nature of evil (and to show why it does not follow):

1. God created all things.
2. Evil is not a thing.
3. Hence God did not create evil.

Some illustrations will help us understand how evil is not a thing in itself but is a lack or corruption in a good thing. Evil is real—a real lack, a real corruption. But it is not a real thing (substance).

Evil Is Like a Wound in an Arm

It is real to have a wound. But a wound is not a "thing." Rather, wounds only exist in good things—like an arm. The wound is real—ask anyone who's had one—but the wound does not exist in itself. It exists only in something else as a privation or corruption of it. Thus there is no such thing as a totally wounded body. A *totally* wounded body is not a body at all.

Evil Is Like Rot to a Tree

Evil is like rottenness in a tree. Here again, pure rottenness exists only in something else. A totally rotten tree is no tree at all—it's topsoil! Rot exists in the tree as a corruption of it, but it does not exist in and of itself.

Evil Is Like Rust to a Car

Rust is a corruption of a good thing (iron), but rust does not exist in and of itself. It is a privation or lack in a good thing. A totally rusted car does not exist; it's just a brown spot on the pavement. Nonetheless, rust is real—it's a real lack in a good thing, as anyone who's had a very rusty car knows.

Evil Is Like Moth Holes in Wool

Moths can corrupt a woolen sweater, but holes do not exist in themselves. They exist only in other things. Again, a totally moth-eaten garment has ceased to exist. Evil is a real corruption, but it is not a real thing (substance).

ANSWERING SOME MISUNDERSTANDINGS

Several misunderstandings have arisen from this explanation of evil's nature. We'll discuss some of them briefly.

Evil Is Not a Mere Absence of Good

In reference to evil as a privation or lack in a good thing, some have wrongly concluded that this makes evil a mere absence of good. But that is not so. For example, the power of sight is absent in rocks and in blind persons, yet there is a big difference.

The stone by nature is not supposed to see, so there is no

privation of sight in it. On the other hand, a human by nature is supposed to see—it's part of his/her nature. In a human being, to be blind is a real privation or lack.

Viewing Evil as a Privation Does Not Imply That Evil Is Unreal

To say evil is a privation, or a lack of some good that ought to be there, does not mean evil is unreal. Privations are real. It is real to be blind. Ask any blind person. Or, try blindfolding yourself.

Likewise, to be maimed (deprived of a limb) is real. It is a real lack. Tie an arm or two behind your back and try performing your normal duties and you will quickly see how real it is to have this privation.

Hence a mere absence is not an evil, but an absence of a good that should be there is an evil. Privations are not *nothing*. They are real—real lacks or corruptions in something that should be there.

Viewing Evil as a Privation Does Not Deny Total Depravity

Biblical Christians believe that fallen human beings are "totally depraved." But we have just seen that nothing can be totally evil. How can this be reconciled?

First of all, the Bible speaks of total depravity in a *moral* sense, not in a *metaphysical* or ontological sense. That is, there cannot be a being that is totally deprived of its being, for then it would be a nonbeing (nothing) and not a being. However, there can be (and are) human beings—all of us—whose beings are totally bent on sinning. We can be totally bent on sinning and still exist. The "total" evil is moral. It has to do with our *intending, willing,* and/or *doing* evil things—not with our very nature as totally deprived of all *being.*

Furthermore, even total depravity in the moral sense does not mean we sin as much as we can all the time. It means we have the propensity (inclination) to sin and the necessity to die (Romans 3, 5). It means we have total inability to attain our own salvation (Ephesians 2:8–9). It does not mean we don't exist as beings in God's image—fallen as we are. The Bible speaks of fallen human beings as still being made in the image of God; this is why it's wrong to murder human beings (Genesis 9:6) or curse them (James 3:9).

What About Satan? Isn't He Totally Evil?

The Bible speaks about Satan as "the evil one" (1 John 5:19) who is a liar by his very nature (John 8:44). Surely there is no good in Satan—is he not totally evil? Yes, he is completely evil in a moral sense, but not in a metaphysical sense. Just like fallen humans still have God's image, even so Satan has the remnants of good that God gave to him as a created angel. For example, Satan has good insofar as he is a creature of God, insofar as he has intelligence, and power, and free will. Of course, he uses all these God-given good powers to do evil; he is ever, always, irretrievably bent on evil. But this is only to say he is totally depraved morally, not that he is totally deprived of all creaturely good metaphysically.

THE PROBLEM OF GOD'S SOVEREIGNTY

Even if evil is not a thing, it's still real, and it's happening. Even if God did not create evil, He does permit it to occur. Hence it may be argued:

1. God is the author (is in sovereign control) of everything that happens.
2. Evil is something that happens.
3. So God is the author of evil.

If this is correct, then even if God is not the author of any evil "thing," would He not still be the author of evil events? In which case, God would still be the author of evil.

In response, we acknowledge that God is in sovereign control. "You can do all things; no plan of yours can be thwarted" (Job 42:2); "Our God is in heaven; he does whatever pleases him" (Psalm 115:3); "The LORD does whatever pleases him, in the heavens and on the earth, in the seas and all their depths" (135:6); "The king's heart is in the hand of the LORD; he directs it like a watercourse wherever he pleases" (Proverbs 21:1). There is nothing that happens apart from God knowing, planning, and controlling it for His purposes. Even the great king Nebuchadnezzar confessed that "the Most High is sovereign over the kingdoms of men and gives them to anyone he wishes and sets over them the lowliest of men" (Daniel 4:17).

Nevertheless, note that the word *author* is being used in two different senses. Yes, God is the author of everything, including evil, in the sense that He *permits* it, but not in the sense that He *produces* it. Evil happens in His *permissive* will, but He does not promote evil in His *perfect* will. God allows evil yet does not encourage it. Just like parents give limited freedom to their children to learn from their mistakes, even so God does with His children. But in no way does God "author" evil in the sense of producing, promoting, or performing it. Indeed, God is "of purer eyes than to see evil and cannot look at wrong" (Habakkuk 1:13 ESV); in His presence, the angels sing "Holy, holy, holy, is the LORD of hosts" (Isaiah 6:3 KJV); "Let no one say when he is tempted, 'I am being tempted by God,' for God cannot be tempted with evil, and he himself tempts no one" (James 1:13 ESV).

God's role in the world is similar to that of a book's "author." He wrote the whole story in advance (Isaiah 46:10); the story has the hero, whom He commends, and the villain, whom He condemns. Each character—whether for good or evil—acts freely, for the story is not about robots, but about humans. So while the author is the author of the villain's actions, the villain is making them freely and is responsible for them. Likewise, God is the author of all human actions, but He is not responsible for them since they are freely chosen. God does not promote or perform the evil actions of His creatures; He merely permits them within the overall story of human history, which He has authored in advance and which moves forward under His sovereign direction.

A good example is the crucifixion of Christ. The Bible says God predetermined that Jesus would be the lamb slain before the creation of the world (Revelation 13:8). Peter said, "This Jesus [was] delivered up according to the definite plan and foreknowledge of God" (Acts 2:23 ESV). But even though the cross was predestined by God, nonetheless, it was freely chosen by Christ: "I lay down my life that I may take it up again. No one takes it from me, but I lay it down of my own accord" (John 10:17–18 ESV). In short, God is the "author" of everything that happens in the indirect and ultimate sense; He is not the immediate cause of evil actions. He neither promotes them nor produces them; He permits them and controls the course of history so that it accomplishes His ultimate purposes. Just as Joseph told his brothers who left him for dead, "You intended to harm me, but God intended it for good" (Genesis 50:20), even so God overrules the evil intent of humans to accomplish His ultimate good.

Of course, explaining evil as a lack in a good thing does not explain where the lack comes from. All it explains is the nature of evil as a real privation in good things. Where the corruption came from is another question—one treated in the next chapter.

Chapter 3

The Origin of Evil

As a pastor, I found that little children ask the toughest questions. One I've been asked many times is "Who made God?" So important is this question that Ravi Zacharias and I wrote a book by that title that has now gone through more than twenty-five printings. Another is "Where did evil come from?" It could not have come from God because He is absolutely good. And how can perfect beings—the only kind God can make—do evil?

God did not create any evil thing. He created only good things, and evil is a privation or corruption of a good thing. No things (substances) are evil in themselves. But this leads inevitably to the mysterious and difficult question: Where, then, did evil come from? That is, how did the privations or corruptions get there?

THE PROBLEM OF EVIL'S ORIGIN

If God is absolutely perfect, and if everything He made is absolutely perfect, then how did evil get off the ground to begin with? How can absolute good be the source of evil? This, indeed, is a great mystery. The problem can be summarized as follows:

1. God is absolutely perfect.
2. God cannot create anything imperfect.
3. A perfect creature cannot do evil.
4. Therefore, evil cannot arise in such a world.
5. But evil did arise in this world.
6. Hence it seems that either premise 1 or 2 (or both) is false, i.e.:
   a. God is not absolutely perfect
   b. God did not create perfect creatures—or
   c. Both a. and b. are true.

Another way to see the problem, in biblical terms, is this: Why didn't God create better creatures—creatures who would not sin? Perhaps if He had made a better Lucifer and better angels, they would not have fallen (Revelation 12:4). After all, two-thirds of the angels did not sin. Why didn't God just create these angels whom He knew in advance would not sin? Why couldn't God have made a better Adam—one who would not have taken the forbidden fruit? After all, the Bible says there will be no sin in heaven (1 Corinthians 13:10; Revelation 21:4). Why did He not create a heaven with only these kinds of creatures to begin with?

RESPONSE TO THE PROBLEM OF EVIL'S ORIGIN

In the above argument, the first two premises seem solid:

1. God is absolutely perfect.
2. God cannot create anything imperfect.

Certainly from an orthodox biblical point of view there is no real ground for denying that God is absolutely perfect. Nor is there any basis for denying that God must make perfect creatures. However, read again the third premise:

3. And a perfect creature cannot do evil.

From a Christian perspective, this is clearly false. God created a perfect archangel, called Lucifer; he sinned (1 Timothy 3:6) and became the devil. *How* can a perfect creature do evil? The answer is *free will*. Consider:

1. God created only good things.
2. One good thing God created was free will.
3. Free will makes evil possible, since
   a. It is the power to do otherwise.
   b. To do otherwise than good is evil.
4. Hence a perfect free creature can do evil.

Certainly God created only good things. Evil cannot come directly from the hand of the Creator any more than polluted water can come directly from a pure mountain spring.

Neither can we deny that free will (the power of free choice) is a good thing. There is nothing evil about it. If there were, then it would be evil for God to have it. And it would be evil for the saints in heaven to have it. But it is not.

The fact is, it's good to be free. No one ever marches against freedom, chanting, "Down with liberty! Back to bondage! I want to do only what the government tells me to do!" Even if someone attempted to speak against freedom, he would be speaking for it, since he believes it's good to be free to express that view. That freedom is good is literally undeniable.

But if it is good to be free, then evil is possible. Freedom means the power to choose otherwise. So in this present world if one is free to do good, he is also free to do evil. If one is free to love, he also is free to hate. If we are free to praise God, then we must be free to curse God. The very nature of our divinely given freedom makes evil possible. Any alleged "freedom" not to choose evil rather than good is not really freedom for a moral creature.

Apart from the saints in heaven (who have it relatively), only God absolutely has the freedom not to choose evil. The highest freedom is the freedom *from* evil, not the freedom *of* doing evil. Here on earth, while we're still making our ultimate choice as to whether we'll do our will or God's will, we must have choice; otherwise we would be robots, puppets, or automatons.

WHO CAUSED LUCIFER TO SIN?

According to the Bible, Lucifer (Isaiah 14:12; cf. 1 Timothy 3:6), a created archangel, was the first to sin, thus becoming Satan. A third of all the angels fell with him (Revelation 12:4). After that, Adam and Eve were tempted by the devil (Genesis 3) and fell into sin (Romans 5:12). There had been no sin in the universe. There was a perfect God, a perfect place called heaven filled with perfect creatures called angels. How could sin arise under such perfect conditions? Who caused Lucifer to sin? He was not tempted by anyone else. God does not tempt anyone to sin (James 1:13). Lucifer had no evil nature that gave him a propensity (inclination) to sin. Many consider this an insoluble mystery. But is it? Not really, not once we understand what free choice entails.

The best way to comprehend the basis of a free act is to examine the three possible alternatives. A free act is either uncaused,

caused by another, or self-caused. That is, it is undetermined, determined by another, or self-determined.

No action can be uncaused (undetermined); that would be a violation of the law of causality (every event has a cause). Neither can a free act be caused by another; for if someone or something else caused the action, then it is not ours (not from our free choice) and we would not be responsible for it. Hence all free actions must be self-caused, that is, caused by oneself.

Now we can answer the question, "What caused Lucifer to sin?" No one did. He is the cause of his own sin. Sin is a self-caused action, one for which we cannot blame anyone or anything else. Who caused the first sin? Lucifer. How did he cause it? By the power of free choice, which God gave him. Thus God made evil *possible* by creating free creatures; they are responsible for making it *actual*.

Some have defined free will in a deterministic sense that leads to a contradiction of God's character. They claim free will means "doing what we desire" and that God must give one the desire to do good, otherwise, by our fallen nature, we do only what is evil. However, this has serious problems. First, why would God give only some, not all, the desire to do good? By this definition, all persons would do good if only God gave them the desire. Further, Lucifer had no fallen nature, so this definition of *freedom* would not explain his evil choice. Surely, no one who believes in an all-good God, who wants all to do good, could consistently claim that God gave Lucifer the desire to rebel against Him. Perish the thought!

Some time ago my wife, Barbara, and I were at a banquet. The speaker, a well-known Christian leader who had lost his son, shared about the difficulty of his struggle to fathom why it happened. He concluded, "I simply could not come to grips with his death until I realized that God killed my son!"

I said quietly to my wife, "I wonder what he would have said if his daughter had been raped?" No, God does not sin, nor does He encourage anyone else to do so. Lucifer sinned on his own, by his own free will.

How Did Evil Arise in a Totally Good Universe?

The Christian defense of free will goes something like this: Evil arose when:

1. A good creature (Lucifer),
2. With the good power of free will,
3. Willed the finite good of the creature (himself)
4. Over the infinite good of the Creator.

It is important to note that *no evil need exist in order to will evil*; for example, willing a lesser good can be an evil. Evil is created by a free person (oneself), and such a person does not have to participate in something outside of himself in order to be evil. The evil of willing oneself to take the place of God is an evil in itself. In fact, this is precisely what the Bible says about the first evil act of Lucifer: It was pride. Paul warned Timothy not to put a novice in office "or he may become conceited [prideful] and fall under the same judgment as the devil" (1 Timothy 3:6).

This is pictured vividly in Ezekiel 28, speaking of the fall of the Prince of Tyre (no doubt inspired by the prince and power of the air [see Ephesians 2]):

> You were in Eden, the garden of God; Every precious stone was your covering . . . [and] was in you on the day that you were created. . . . You were on the holy mountain of God; You walked in the midst of the stones of fire. *You were blameless in your ways*

from the day you were created until unrighteousness was found in you. . . . And you sinned; Therefore I have cast you as profane from the mountain of God. And I have destroyed you, *O covering cherub,* from the midst of the stones of fire. *Your heart was lifted up [in pride] because of your beauty;* you corrupted your wisdom by reason of your splendor. (Ezekiel 28:13–17 NASB)

Isaiah paints a similar picture:

How art thou fallen from heaven, O Lucifer, son of the morning! . . . For thou hast said in thine heart, I will ascend into heaven. *I will exalt my throne above the stars of God. . . . I will be like the most High.* (Isaiah 14:12–14 KJV)

Thus sin was born in the breast of an archangel in the presence of God.

A stunningly beautiful and extremely powerful creature fell when he made himself, rather than God, the object of his adoration.

God created only good things. One good thing He made was free will. A good being, with the good power of free will, chose to put his will over God's. Who caused Lucifer to sin? No one else did—he was the cause of his own sin.

Sin is a self-caused action, caused by oneself. Hence it is as meaningless to ask, "Who caused Lucifer to sin?" as it is to ask, "Who made God?" No one made God, the Unmade Maker, and Lucifer is the maker of his own sin.

Chapter 4

The Persistence of Evil

Nothing is worse than watching a loved one die a slow and painful death. I can remember sitting up all night watching one of my parishioners waste away in a torturous demise. Early in the morning we helplessly watched his deep and desperate breathing, only to be replaced by the ominous death-rattle in his throat, the gasping for air, and the final gulp.

The only thing worse is to watch a little child die and futilely attempt to comfort her parents. Then later, to stand by at the gravesite as they throw the last shovels of dirt on the tiny coffin. One funeral we had was of both parents and little children, hit broadside on their way home from a Wednesday night prayer meeting.

No one with an ounce of kindness could wish such tragedies on anyone. And yet God seems to stand idly by His creation and watch this kind of thing happen all the time. Every kind and merciful heart cries out, "*Why?* Why doesn't God stop it all?"

Why does He not call a halt to all suffering? Better yet, when evil first broke out, why didn't He nip the whole thing in the bud? He has the power to do so. Does He lack the compassion?

Even granting the explanation for the *nature* of evil as a

privation of good (chapter 2) and of free will as the *origin* of the privation (chapter 3), the painful question remains as to evil's *persistence*. In other words, when Lucifer and the angels rebelled, why didn't God squash wickedness then and there? Why doesn't He do it today? Surely an all-powerful God could end the whole thing now.

THE PROBLEM OF EVIL'S PERSISTENCE STATED

The argument from the persistence of evil is one of the oldest and most difficult of all arguments against God. It has been used by skeptics from time immemorial.

Briefly put, either God cannot abolish evil or He will not. If He cannot, then He isn't all-powerful; if He will not, then He isn't all-good. Logically, it can be stated as follows:

1. If God is all-good, He would destroy evil.
2. If God is all-powerful, He could destroy evil.
3. But evil is not destroyed.
4. Therefore, no such God exists.

Of course, this is not an argument against all views of God, but an argument against the Christian (theistic) view of an infinitely powerful and all-loving God. A finite god who's not all-powerful and/or all-good might exist, but not an infinitely good and infinitely powerful God.

However, this view has serious issues of its own. How could one know God was imperfect unless there was some ultimate standard of perfection by which he could measure this finite "god" as not perfect? Further, since every finite being needs a cause, then the cause of such a finite, imperfect god would have to be a perfect, infinite Being (God). Finally, a finite god cannot guarantee the ultimate overthrow of evil; only an all-powerful God can.

Nonetheless, the above argument poses a serious problem for the theistic God. Let's look at the premises carefully. The Christian theist has no dispute with the first premise. God *is* all-good and, as such, He surely desires to do away with evil. After all, it is contrary to His very essential, unchanging nature (Leviticus 11:45; Isaiah 6:3; Malachi 3:6; James 1:17; Hebrews 1:10–12; 6:18).

The second premise seems solid as well. God is "the almighty God" (Genesis 17:1; Job 5:17), the Lord God omnipotent (Revelation 19:6 NKJV). "Nothing is impossible for God," (Luke 1:37), so would it not follow that He could do away with evil? Hence evil's persistence seems to fly in the face of God—at least the God of the Bible.

A RESPONSE TO THE ARGUMENT FROM EVIL'S PERSISTENCE

There are two basic responses. The first challenges a popular misconception of God's omnipotence (all-powerfulness), along with an equivocation on the word *destroy*. Is it really possible to destroy evil without destroying freedom? It would seem not, at least in the strong sense of the word *destroy*; at least it would be incompatible with God's love.

God Can't Destroy Evil Without Destroying Freedom

Let's look carefully at the second premise: "If God is all-powerful, He could destroy evil." If *destroy* is understood in the strong sense of "totally obliterate," then there is a serious problem with it. It's not literally true that God can do *anything*. For instance, He can't cease being God. He can't change. "It is impossible for

God to lie" (Hebrews 6:18) or go against His own nature. God cannot make a square circle or round triangle. God can't make a stone so heavy that He can't lift it, for anything He makes must be finite, and an infinite God has no problem lifting a finite stone. So more properly speaking, omnipotence means God can do anything that is *possible* to do, not what is impossible or contradictory.

Given this understanding of omnipotence, even God cannot totally destroy all evil without destroying freedom. Given that He has willed to create free creatures, it would go against His own will to destroy our free will. So given free will, it is impossible for God to totally destroy evil. C. S. Lewis captures this concept well:

> I would pay any price to be able to say truthfully, "All will be saved." But my reason retorts, "Without their will, or with it?" *If I say "Without their will" I at once perceive a contradiction; how can the supreme voluntary act of self-surrender be involuntary?* If I say "With their will," my reason replies, "How, if they will not give in?" (*The Problem of Pain*, 106–107, emphasis added)

There are some things even God cannot do. He cannot *force* anyone to *freely* accept Him. Forced freedom is a contradiction in terms. This is why Jesus said,

> Jerusalem, Jerusalem, you who kill the prophets and stone those sent to you, how often I have longed to gather your children together, as a hen gathers her chicks under her wings, but *you were not willing.* (Matthew 23:37)

So the only way God could literally destroy all evil is to destroy all freedom. However, to destroy all freedom is to destroy the possibility of all moral good. *All moral choices are free choices.* No one can be praised or blamed for an act in which they had no free choice. If they were forced to do it, then they can't get either credit or blame. Hence if God destroyed all freedom, He would be destroying all possibility to love, praise, and worship Him—to say nothing of destroying all possibility of our enjoying His or other people's love, praise, and sacrifice on our behalf.

Further, since God has willed to create free creatures—and it is good to be free—He cannot destroy all evil that comes from free creatures without destroying all the free choices that produce these acts. God's elimination of evil choices we make would take away our freedom, for our freedom in this world involves the ability to do both evil and good. Preventing one of these would be destroying the freedom to do both.

Can God Defeat Evil Without Destroying Freedom?

Does this mean God can *never* defeat evil? No, it doesn't—not if *defeat* isn't understood as implying a destruction of our freedom. For example, if *defeat* means to conquer, triumph over, disable, and/or vanquish evil (without destroying free choice), then there is no contradiction involved. In this sense, the argument against God from the persistence of evil can be restated as follows:

1. If God is all-good, He would defeat evil.
2. If God is all-powerful, He could defeat evil.
3. But evil is not defeated.
4. Therefore, no such God exists.

Now, in this form of the argument, it would appear the first two premises are true. Certainly being all-good, God wants to defeat evil. And if He is all-powerful (and can do whatever is possible to do), then there must be some way He can overcome evil without destroying freedom. If not, then why create free creatures to begin with? Why waste all of human history on a project He knows will fail?

Since God is omniscient (all-knowing), knowing "the end from the beginning" (Isaiah 46:10), and since He has set aside a plan of redemption, including the death of His only Son (Revelation 13:8; Acts 2:23), and since He "chose us in Him before the creation of the world" (Ephesians 1:4), and since He infallibly predicts a victorious end of the world (Revelation 21–22; 1 Corinthians 15:25–28), then *surely He has a plan that includes the defeat of evil without the destruction of freedom.*

Granting this, there still is a serious issue with the revised argument from evil's persistence.

The real problem then is in the third premise: "Evil is not defeated." It has no time indicator on it. Since this is an argument in the present, it must be restated as follows:

1. If God is all-good, He would defeat evil.
2. If God is all-powerful, He could defeat evil.
3. But evil is not *yet* defeated.
4. Therefore, no such God exists.

When the argument is put in form, the conclusion doesn't follow from the premises. Evil may yet be defeated in the future. It simply does not follow that because God has not yet defeated evil He never will. To claim so is like saying that because a speaker has not yet come to a conclusion in his lecture he never will. Give him a chance. Listen to the whole thing. History is not over. Let's wait to hear "the rest of the story."

We have no infallible knowledge of the future. Given who God is—keep in mind that He is all-powerful and all-good— we have every right to expect that He will defeat evil (we'll look more at this in chapters 5 and 6).

THE FINAL REVISION OF THE ARGUMENT ALSO FAILS

Of course the atheist can revise his argument. All he has to do is add a phrase to the third premise, and then the whole thing will look like this:

1. If God is all-good, He would defeat evil.
2. If God is all-powerful, He could defeat evil.
3. But evil is not *yet* defeated, *and it never will be defeated.*
4. Therefore, no such God exists.

Now the argument is valid (in that the conclusion follows from the premises), but the third premise cannot be established by any mortal mind. Hence the conclusion does not follow. Only God knows the future infallibly; only He can foresee whether evil will or will not one day be defeated. In order for the atheist to know the third premise is true, he would have to be God; that is, he would have to be omniscient (all-knowing). Thus, the argument from evil's persistence does not eliminate a theistic God.

THE BOOMERANG EFFECT OF THE ARGUMENT FROM EVIL'S PERSISTENCE

There is in fact a boomerang effect from this argument against God. Given the premises, it actually turns out to be an argument in favor of evil's defeat.

If such a theistic God exists, and there is good evidence that He does (see appendix 2), then evil eventually will be defeated. How do we know? Because if God is all-good, He wants to defeat it, and if He is all-powerful, He is able to defeat it. Therefore, evil *will* one day be defeated. Consider the following.

1. If there is an all-good God, He wants to defeat evil.
2. If there is an all-powerful God, He can defeat evil.
3. But evil is not *yet* defeated.
4. Therefore, *evil will one day be defeated.*

The first two premises we already have examined and accepted. The third seems obvious, but let's examine it more carefully. Is it true that "evil is not yet defeated"? Maybe the world can't get any better than it is. If so, then maybe in some weak sense of the word *defeat* the victory has already come.

HAS EVIL ALREADY BEEN DEFEATED?

It would seem this answer is logically possible. That is, the present state of affairs in relation to good and evil may be the very best it can be. If so, then evil has already been "defeated," and we have our answer: God has defeated evil without destroying our freedom. According to some versions of this view, evil is as necessary to an overall picture of God as ugly little pieces of stone are necessary to the overall beauty of a mosaic. Or evil is as necessary for an overall good as dark places in a painting are necessary to bring out the beauty of lighter areas.

Even though this view is logically possible, it actually seems unsatisfactory for several reasons. Certainly, from this perspective, God has not destroyed our freedom, but neither has He defeated evil. There seem to be several reasons to think this view is not true.

First, *metaphysically*, this view involves calling evil good, for the evil "parts" are said to be a part of the "whole" good. But we have seen (in chapter 2) that there are no evil things—parts or wholes. Evil is a privation or corruption of good things.

Second, *logically*, this current world does not appear to be the best of all possible worlds (namely, the one where good has triumphed and evil is defeated). Anyone can easily think of a better world. For example, a world with one less rape or one less murder would be a better world. And there is no reason to believe this is not actually possible.

Third, *morally,* this world lacks the qualities necessary to qualify for the word *defeat* to apply to evil. Evil is still on the rampage, both morally and physically. Hatred, crime, and war have not been significantly diminished. More powerful weapons have made it possible to destroy more people. Nor have tornados, earthquakes, and hurricanes vanished. This says nothing of suffering, poverty, and starvation. It seems intuitively obvious that there could be a much better world than this one. If not, the word *omnipotent* (all-powerful) as applied to God has been deprived of significant meaning.

Frankly, if this present world is the best it can get, then a finite god would seem to be a sufficient explanation for it.

Anyone not convinced this isn't the best of all possible worlds might read the classic satire on this thesis by Voltaire, titled *Candide.*

"Master, we have come to beg you to tell us why so strange an animal as man was ever created." "What has it to do with you?" said Dervish. "Is it your business?" "But, reverend father," said Candide, "there is a horrible amount of evil in the world." "What does it matter?" said Dervish, "whether there is evil or good? When his highness sends a ship to Egypt, does he worry about the comfort or discomfort of the rats in the ship?" "Then what should we do?" said Pangloss. "Hold your tongue," said the Dervish. "I flatter myself," said Pangloss, "that I should discuss with you effects and causes, this best of all possible worlds . . . and preestablished harmony." At these words the Dervish slammed the door in their faces. (187)

It seems obvious that a world in which evil is "defeated" would have a greater sense of victory and security from evil than this one. Indeed, according to the Bible this victory over evil will involve several factors: Physical evils will be banished (Romans 8:18–21; Revelation 21:1–4); moral evils will be separated and quarantined so they can no longer spread (Matthew 25:31–46; Revelation 20:11–15); each person, whether good or evil, will be separated according to his free choice (Matthew 23:37; 2 Thessalonians 1:7–9; no one will be forced to any destiny against his will); and sin will no longer be possible among the redeemed— our freedom will be perfected and fulfilled (1 Corinthians 13:12; Revelation 21:1–5).

If this biblically projected picture occurs someday, then there will be sufficient ground for believing evil has been "defeated" without freedom being destroyed (see chapter 7). Meanwhile, all evidence for a theistic God (see appendix 2) is also evidence for an ultimate defeat of evil.

As persuasive as the argument from evil's persistence may seem to be, in the end it turns out to be a failure. That God has not yet defeated evil does *not* mean He never will. Further, if God is all-good (wants to defeat evil) and all-powerful (can defeat evil), then it is a certainty that evil will one day be defeated. Why? Because God can and wants to do it; therefore, He will. There simply is no logical way to refute this conclusion. In addition, if God is omniscient (all-knowing), then surely He knows whether evil will be defeated. It is highly unlikely, given these attributes, that God would have created such a world as ours if He did not know in advance that evil would be defeated. And this is exactly what the Bible says He will do.

Chapter 5

The Purpose of Evil

My first pastorate was a small rural charge in the rolling hills of Tuscola County, Michigan. Our closest neighbor, half a mile down the road, was the Harp family. Mrs. Harp and the four Harp children were always faithful in attending church. Mr. Harp was too busy for God. The cows and the farm demanded attention—though most of the other farmers managed to attend to both their earthly and heavenly duties.

One day Mrs. Harp was taken to the hospital. When I arrived and asked for her, the nurse at the desk said, "Mrs. Harp has expired." I hurried back to the Harp residence to comfort Mr. Harp and make plans for the funeral. I also asked him if I could borrow his wife's Bible to find her favorite verse to use for the service.

As soon as I got back home, I opened it and saw these words written in fresh ink: "I am content to leave my loved ones in thy hands, O God, knowing that your love for them is greater than my own!" I couldn't believe it. I jumped in my car and returned to show Mr. Harp what very well could have been her last words. After sharing them, I said, "Your wife was a believer, and she is in heaven with Jesus. Would you like to receive Christ and be with her in His presence someday?"

Mr. Harp bowed his head and accepted Christ as His Savior. After that, each Sunday he joined his four children and sat in the pew his departed loved one had once occupied. The words of Mrs. Harp still ring in my ears: "I am content to leave my loved ones in thy hands, O God, knowing that your love for them is greater than my own!" We don't always see God's purposes worked out so quickly on earth. Sometimes we won't see until we reach the other side. But God has His purposes nonetheless.

We already have discussed evil's nature (chapter 2), origin (chapter 3), and persistence (chapter 4). We turn our attention now to its purpose. The question can be put many ways with many different connotations. For instance, what is the significance of suffering? What is the meaning of misery? What is the cause for calamity? Or what is the purpose of pain?

PROBLEM: THERE SEEMS TO BE NO APPARENT PURPOSE FOR SOME EVIL

Most people have experienced what seems like purposeless pain. Many of us have undergone experiences where there is no discernible significance for the suffering. And the question *Why?* lingers in our mind. To put it in a more logical form:

1. An all-good God must have a good purpose for everything.
2. But there is no good purpose for some (i.e., useless or innocent) suffering.
3. Hence there cannot be an all-good God.

Initially, note that this argument does not eliminate all views of God, only the theistic view. There might be a finite god who is limited in either his goodness or power, but the inadequacies of that view have been addressed already (in chapter 4). Clearly, this is not the biblical view of God. So the conclusion, if true, would argue against the God of the Bible.

The theist grants the first premise. God is all-good, and an all-good God must have good purposes for all. That is, He cannot have a bad purpose for anything, and He must have a good purpose for everything. If He didn't, then He wouldn't be an all-good God.

It is the second premise that is problematic for theism. Indeed, it plainly seems to be wrong, as will be shown below. It does not follow logically to conclude that (1) our *knowing* no purpose and (2) there actually *being* no purpose are the same.

RESPONSE TO THE ARGUMENT FROM THE APPARENT PURPOSELESSNESS FOR SOME EVIL

Noted thinkers have pointed out the logical fallacy in the second premise's reasoning and, thus, the fallacy of the conclusion drawn from it. Simply put, *that we don't know a good purpose for some evil does not mean there is no good purpose for it.* There are many things we don't know. And there are many things we once did not know but now do know. So it should be expected that in the future we will discover good purposes for things for which we do not now know a good purpose.

Added to this is the fact that we have later experienced learning things that once we could not explain. This gives us reasonable confidence that in the future we will be able to explain good purposes for evils we cannot now explain.

Take an illustration from science. Evolutionists once

claimed there were some one hundred eighty vestigial organs (with no known function) left over from our animal ancestry. Over the last century or so, this list has shrunk to six! And now there are known functions even for these. More recently some scientists were speaking of "junk genes," but now there are good reasons for believing they have a special function—playing, for example, a key role in controlling gene expression (see Stephen Meyer, *Signature in the Cell*, 406–407). Further, even *Nature* magazine (2009) refers to them as "the junk that makes us human" as they account for the crucial differences among species. In fact, this is all evidence of intelligent design. Finally, to *assume* they are junk is to hinder scientific research.

Here again, further study has shown that the unexplained is not necessarily the unexplainable. Likewise, that we don't know a good purpose for some suffering does not mean there is none.

It Should Not Be Expected That We Know the Purpose for Everything

Further, it should not be expected that finite minds would know the real purpose for everything, including all evils in the world. After all, we are by nature limited in our knowledge. We don't know everything, so it should come as no surprise that we don't know the reason for all suffering. This by no means is the same as saying there is no reason for apparently inexplicable suffering.

Certainly, it's not a shock to the Christian that we cannot explain all the world's suffering. God informs us that "The secret things belong to the LORD our God" (Deuteronomy 29:29). Paul marveled of God, "How unsearchable are his judgments and how inscrutable his ways!" (Romans 11:33 ESV). In his encounter with Job on this very topic, God said, "Who is this that hides counsel without knowledge?" Job confessed, "I have uttered what I did not understand, things too wonderful for me, which I did not know" (Job 42:3 ESV).

An Infinitely Good Mind Knows a Good Purpose for Everything

Not only can no mortal assert with confidence that there can be no good purpose for some suffering (because we do not know it), but we can affirm with certainty that God does know the good purpose for all suffering and other evils. Why? Because God is omniscient, and an all-knowing mind knows everything. Further, God is omnibenevolent, and an all-good God has a good purpose for everything He does or permits. Hence we know for sure that there is a good purpose for all suffering—including the apparently unjust or innocent kinds—even if we do not know it. Let's summarize this reasoning:

1. That we don't know a good purpose for evil does not mean there is none.
2. An all-good God knows a good purpose for everything (including evil).
   a. Some evil seems to us to have no good purpose.
   b. But an all-good God has a good purpose for everything.
   c. *So even evil that seems to have no good purpose does have a good purpose.*
3. Therefore, there is a good purpose for all suffering, even that which we cannot now explain.

THINGS ONCE UNEXPLAINED BUT NOW EXPLAINED

Scientists cannot currently explain everything in the natural world. But they have good reason to believe that there are explanations for the things they can't explain.

Why? First, the unexplained is not unexplainable. Second, many things they once could not explain (e.g., earthquakes, meteors, hurricanes, and tornados), they can now explain. For these same two reasons, we can believe there is an explanation for suffering we cannot now explain: Unexplained evils are not unexplainable, and many evils we once could not explain we can now explain.

Likewise, many evils have happened in our lives that at the time were inexplicable. Later, however, we saw the hand of God in it all. Certainly Joseph did not know why he was sold as a slave into Egypt by his brothers. Later, however, he was able to say to them: "You meant evil against me, but God meant it for good, to bring it about that many people should be kept alive, as they are today" (Genesis 50:20 ESV). Indeed, "for the moment all discipline seems painful rather than pleasant, but later it yields the peaceful fruit of righteousness to those who have been trained by it" (Hebrews 12:10–11 ESV).

Most of us who have lived any length of time can think of several unhappy incidents that turned out in the end to be for our good. I remember how disappointed my friend Wally was. He had a wife, seven children, and only a low-wage job. Nonetheless, he'd just decided he was going to put God first and begin tithing. Shortly thereafter, his boss called him in to give him the bad news that he was going to be let go. "Someday you're going to thank me for this," he said.

That seemed of little comfort to jobless Wally at the time. However, only a few months later he found a similar job that paid twice as much. Of course, not all who are faithful are rewarded so fully and quickly, but the point is the same: Even when we don't know a good purpose for an event, there is one.

A PLACE FOR REASONABLE FAITH

Even though we do not always know why, *at least we know why we do not know why*—because we are limited in our knowledge. God isn't, and He wants us to trust Him. Further, we not only know why we don't know why, but we know the One who does know why: an infinitely good God. Thus, we have faith—supported by good reason for knowing a theistic God exists (see appendix 2)—in the God who does know why. And we can trust Him when we don't know why, because we know He does.

Abraham had reason to believe God was just. Therefore, he had no problem leaving the judgment of Sodom and Gomorrah to God with these words: "Will not the Judge of all the earth do right?" (Genesis 18:25). Likewise, Job did not understand why he was suffering, yet even after he had lost everything he was able to say, "The LORD gave and the LORD has taken away; may the name of the LORD be praised" (Job 1:21). This is faith, but it is not an unreasonable faith. Whatever good reasons we have for believing that God is God (i.e., infinitely good, knowing, and powerful), we also have for believing that He has a good purpose for allowing the suffering He allows.

The late great radio announcer Paul Harvey once visited a young man dying of terminal cancer. Despite the fact that his vibrant life and bright future were being tragically interrupted by what seemed to be a premature death, he said to Paul: *"I do not believe the Divine Architect of the universe ever builds a staircase that leads to nowhere."* Granted the good reasons to believe that there is a divine Designer of this universe, this is a reasonable faith.

Anyone who has read the books of quadriplegic Joni Eareckson Tada knows how a diving accident as a teenager destroyed the function of all four of her limbs for life. They also know God's triumph in this tragedy through her vibrant and radiant faith. In *A Step Further,* she declares:

> What a mistake to think that I would ever be able to complete the whole puzzle of suffering. For wisdom is more than just seeing our problems through God's eyes—it is also trusting Him even when the pieces don't seem to fit. (172)

WE DO KNOW SOME GOOD PURPOSES FOR PAIN AND SUFFERING

Not only is our faith justified in believing that God has a purpose for things that seem purposeless (because of the evidence for His very existence and nature), but we also know from experience that there are good purposes for much of the pain we humans endure. This gives us confidence to believe there are good purposes for the rest that we are now unable to fully explain.

There are many things we suffer for which we do know a good purpose. For example, warning pains. A toothache is a good pain that warns us of something worse and gives us a chance to correct the problem. Likewise, a sharp pain in the chest can be a warning of a potentially fatal heart attack. A pain in the lower right side can prevent death by a burst appendix. There are in fact many lessons we can learn from pain.

Lesson One: Pain is designed to keep us from self-destruction.

Medical science has discovered that the body's nervous system that conveys pain to us is designed to save our lives.

Scientific research on leprosy has revealed that most of the loss of fingers and toes is not caused by the disease but by the leper himself. Leprosy destroys the ability to sense pain. Hence the leper has no warning when he is in dangerous situations that can cause harm or even death to his body. For example, if one cannot feel pain, then he could be severely or fatally burned without even knowing it.

Lesson Two: In order to save us from self-destruction the pain has to be strong enough.

In addition, experiments done with lepers demonstrate some of pain's main purposes. When lepers were equipped with bleeping devices to warn of pain, it was discovered that they did not work. Why? Because a bleep is not painful, it did not divert them from unwitting self-destructive activity.

Lesson Three: In order for pain to work it has to be out of our control.

Further, doctors learned that hooking up a shock mechanism did not work either. Once the leper learned he would be shocked by a sharp warning pain in certain situations, he would turn the system off so as not to be confronted with it again. Now, it is difficult to imagine a better way to utilize pain for our benefit than the world in which we live. Certainly the pain is strong enough, and it is often beyond our control. Rabbi Harold Kushner admitted this point in *When Bad Things Happen to Good People*: "I am a more sensitive person, a more effective pastor, a more sympathetic counselor because of [my son] Aaron's life and death than I would have ever been without it" (133). But he added, "If I could choose, I would forgo all the spiritual growth and depth which has come my way" (ibid.). And that is the point: None of us will to go through suffering, and yet most of us admit we are better persons for having done so.

There is nothing more out of our control than death, and there is nothing more painful than the death of a child. I know, because I have experienced it. As a pastor of some forty years, I thought I had seen everything. I buried my sister. I buried my father. I buried my mother. But when my daughter died a tragic death, I was totally crushed. I could not stop crying. I couldn't stop saying, "What a waste! What a waste! What a waste!" I could see no good purpose in it all. But God could, and He was more than ready to show me.

The tears had hardly dried on my cheeks when a student sat silently in my office, just looking at me (she was trying to catch some glimpse of how I was coming to grips with the tragedy). Suddenly, she broke the silence: "My mother committed suicide." A week or so later, an administrator entered my office, sat in the chair by my desk, and with no introduction blurted out, "My father committed suicide." In the past few years I can't tell you how many people God has brought into my life who've had the same experience. Nor can I tell how much the words of Paul have etched themselves on my heart:

> Praise be to the God and Father of our Lord Jesus Christ, the Father of compassion and the God of all comfort, who comforts us in all our troubles, so that we can comfort those in any trouble with the comfort we ourselves have received from God. (2 Corinthians 1:3–4)

If for no other reason, God sometimes allows us to suffer pain so that we can comfort others suffering in a like situation.

C. S. Lewis succinctly noted another purpose in *The Problem of Pain*: "God whispers to us in our pleasures, speaks in our conscience, but *[God] shouts in our pain: it is his megaphone to rouse a deaf world"* (81, emphasis added). The truth is that we learn more enduring lessons through pain than we do pleasure. There is no Bible verse that says, "I am happy; be ye happy, says the Lord." There *are* verses that say, "Be holy because I, the LORD your God, am holy" (Leviticus 19:2). And since God is a moral being who made us moral beings like Himself and wants us to be morally perfect like Himself (Matthew 5:48), it is understandable that He would be more interested in our character than our comfort; more concerned about our holiness than our happiness. And given that pain is such an effective means in developing character (Romans 5:2–4; James 1:2–3; 2 Corinthians 4:17), it should be no surprise that God has provided a suitable training ground conducive to our moral development. In fact, as Lewis muses, given the effectiveness of pain in producing moral gain, it is surprising that there is not more pain. So the question should not be why there is *so much* pain, but why is there not *more?*

WHAT GOD DOES THROUGH ALLOWING SUFFERING

"No pain, no gain" is not just a popular slogan, it is a moral postulate (cf. Genesis 50:20). Again, consider what the Scriptures say: "No discipline seems pleasant at the time, but painful. Later on, however, it produces a harvest of righteousness" (Hebrews 12:11). "Count it all joy, my brothers, when you meet trials of various kinds, for you know that the testing of your faith produces steadfastness" (James 1:2–3 ESV). "We also rejoice in our sufferings, because we know that suffering produces perseverance; perseverance, character; and character, hope" (Romans 5:3–4).

Many years ago I was in a hospital, dying of hepatitis. I'd just been married, and there I was lying next to a man dying of a heart attack. The radio in the room blared that a famous senator had just died of hepatitis. I was not feeling well when someone sent me a card that read:

Overheard in an Orchard

Said the Robin to the Sparrow,
"I should really like to know
Why these anxious human beings
Rush about and worry so."
Said the Sparrow to the Robin,
"Friend, I think that it must be
That they have no heavenly Father
Such as cares for you and me."

—Elizabeth Cheney

SUMMING UP THE SITUATION

An *all-knowing* God knows the end of all things. An *all-good* God wants to bring all things to a good end. And an *all-powerful* God can bring all things to a good end. Therefore, all things (including suffering we don't understand) will come to a good end—if not in this life, then in the next. In short, only the biblical, theistic God guarantees a good end. Bad things will happen to good people, but a good God has for us a good end, for these bad things will bring about good results: "Our light and momentary troubles are achieving for us an eternal glory that far outweighs them all" (2 Corinthians 4:17).

Chapter 6

The Avoidability of Evil

If we knew in advance that we would have a son who would become Adolf Hitler or Osama bin Laden, wouldn't it be better not to conceive him to begin with? If we knew the building we were erecting would collapse and kill thousands of people, wouldn't it be better not to build it? Likewise, I am often asked, "If God knew in advance that all this evil would happen, why did He create the world? Wouldn't *nothing* be better than something evil? Or better yet, why didn't He create a better world—one where evil would not occur?"

If we answer that "Evil is necessary to achieve greater goods," then why not a world where everyone (not just some) achieves these greater goods? Why this world where most evils don't achieve a greater good? Further, there appear to have been many alternatives open to God that would seem better than this one that involves so much evil. Why then did God not choose to make a better world? Or more pointedly, how could God be all-good, all-powerful, and all-knowing and make this kind of world?

THE PROBLEM OF EVIL'S AVOIDABILITY

According to Christian theism, God is not only all-powerful, all-good, and all-knowing, but He is also free. That is, He *chose* to make this world. He did not have to make it, but He willed to do so. Indeed, there was no one else and nothing else there to force Him to do so. Nor was there any lack in His nature—He is absolutely perfect (Matthew 5:48) and self-contained (Acts 17:24–25)—that drove Him to do so. John said, "You created all things, and *by your will they existed and were created*" (Revelation 4:11 ESV). In His omniscience He knew exactly what would happen, since He knows "the end from the beginning" (Isaiah 46:10).

This poses a pointed problem, namely, why did God make a world that He knew would go this bad? Did not even Jesus say of Judas, who betrayed Him, "It would be better for him if he had not been born" (Matthew 26:24)? It doesn't take much imagination to conceive of better worlds. God could have made:

1. No world at all;
2. A world with no free creatures in it;
3. A world with free creatures who could not sin;
4. A world with free creatures who would not sin;
5. A world with free creatures who would sin, but all would be saved.

In short, there are many better worlds God could have made that are not as bad as this one, and most of them involve no evil at all. Why then did He not make one of them? As the philosopher Wilhelm Gottfried Leibniz reasoned (in *Theodicy*), if God is the best of all possible beings, then He must make the best of all possible worlds. But this world is not the best of all possible worlds; therefore, how can God be the best of all possible beings? If He is not, then the God of the Bible does not exist. This would seem to be a very powerful argument and, as such, it deserves careful attention.

A RESPONSE TO THE "BETTER WORLD" ARGUMENT

The only adequate way to respond is to address each alleged alternative, one by one, to see if any world would have been better than ours.

No World at All Is Not a Morally Better World

It is true that God had a choice to create or not to create. But is it true that not to create is morally better than to create? There are two serious problems with such an assertion.

First, it assumes that nothing is better than something. This is a gigantic category mistake, because being and nonbeing are not in the same category. It simply is not possible that nothing is better than something, since nothing is *nothing,* and something and nothing don't have anything in common. Comparisons like *better than* can only be made where both things have something in common to compare. Thus the statement that nothing is better than something is baseless.

Second, the question at hand is not whether no world is better *metaphysically* (in its being), but whether it is better *morally* than this morally evil world. But here again there is no basis for the comparison: one is a moral world and the other is not a moral world. A nonmoral world cannot be morally better than a moral world, for it is not a moral world at all. This too is a huge category mistake.

What, then, did Jesus mean about Judas? One thing is

certain: He was not asserting (for the above reasons) that the nonbeing of Judas would be morally better than his being. When the statement is examined, even in a literal sense, it is not about Judas's nonbeing but about his pre-birth condition and his post-birth condition. Judas (as well as any other person) existed in his mother's womb before he was born (Psalm 139; 51:5; Matthew 1:20; Luke 1:31, 41). Jesus was not comparing *nothing* to *something*. At best, He was comparing an innocent, painless prenatal state with a sad and tragic post-natal state.

Further, it is not necessary to take Jesus' statement literally. It may be a figure of speech, indicating the severity of Judas's judgment. He is also called "the son of perdition (hell)," which is clearly not a place of nothingness (see chapter 8). Jesus often used figures of speech, such as "I am the true vine" (John 15:1) or "I am the bread of life" (6:35). He even used hyperbole, such as straining a gnat while swallowing a camel (Matthew 23:24). The point of His statement that "it would be better for him if he had not been born" is to stress the greatness of Judas's sin. Indeed, Jesus said that Judas had committed a "greater sin" than Pilate (John 19:11). In brief, neither this nor any other scriptural text supports the thesis that nothing is morally better than something.

A Non-Free World Is Not a Morally Better World

It is true that a world with no free (moral) creatures would have no sin. Rocks, animals, and robots do not sin. Only moral creatures with reason and free will are capable of sinning, for there is no moral responsibility where there is no moral ability to respond. Axes aren't tried for crimes. Rather, a morally responsible person who used an axe to murder is tried and punished for his actions.

So here too is a false comparison. There is no common ground between a nonmoral and a moral world. A nonmoral world may be *physically* better, in that it has no physical evils, but it cannot be said to be *morally* better. It may have no sickness, death, or disasters, but if there are no moral creatures there to suffer them, then being physically free from these conditions does not make it a moral world but rather simply a physically good world. A nonmoral world cannot be morally better than anything.

A Free World Where No One Can Sin Is Not a Morally Better World

Some object that since God is free but cannot sin (Hebrews 6:18; Titus 1:2), it is not contradictory to be free and yet unable to sin. Isn't the highest freedom the freedom from sin (like God has), not the freedom to sin (as we have)? Further, won't we be free from sin in heaven? If so, why didn't God make heaven first? This would have avoided all sin.

In response, freedom, as we have it here on earth, is incompatible with the impossibility to sin. Freedom in this context involves the ability to do otherwise. But if sin is impossible, then one does not have the ability to do otherwise. Hence freedom in the normal sense of the ability to do otherwise (the power of contrary choice) is contradictory to sin being impossible. One cannot at the same time and in the same sense have both the possibility and impossibility to sin.

One may object that the *power* to do otherwise is not the same as *doing* otherwise. Maybe the people in heaven have the ability to sin but not the willingness to do so. There are two problems with this view.

First, if so, then the sin question is not settled, even in

heaven, for then once we get to heaven it is still possible to sin. What is the guarantee that sin will not break out again? This could scarcely be up to the standards for a place of ultimate perfection and happiness. The Bible describes heaven as "perfect" (1 Corinthians 13:10, 12) and sinless (1 John 3:2; Revelation 21:4; 22:3).

Second, on this view, there is no explanation for why heaven can be permanent and perfect, if people still have the ability to sin. The only real guarantee that heaven will remain sinless forever is that it will no longer be possible to sin.

As for the objection that *God* is free but cannot sin, and, therefore, there is no reason why we should not be able to do the same on earth: first, we are not God, and, second, we are not yet in heaven. The highest kind of freedom—a godlike freedom—is the freedom from sin, not the freedom to sin. True, we can become more godlike here, and in heaven we will be as perfectly godlike (1 John 3:2) as creatures can get—including our freedom from sin (Revelation 21–22). But some things cannot be created directly; some things can be produced only through a process. Again, patience is produced through the process of tribulation (Romans 5:3 KJV). Trial forms character (James 1:2), and there can be no sense of forgiveness without sin.

In short, God has to create free creatures who could sin before He could produce free creatures who can't sin. It's like the difference between a shotgun wedding and a marriage freely chosen. In both cases the person is married, but in only one case was it a free choice. Better yet, it is the difference between consensual sex and sexual assault; clearly one is free and the other is not. Since God by His very nature (love) cannot force anyone to love Him, it would be highly improper to think of a heaven where people were forced to be there. First there must be courtship, and then two can be bound together for life. God had to give us lower freedom (freedom to do evil) in order to achieve a higher freedom for us (freedom from evil).

To carry the analogy further, we are bound by our marriage vows to one and only one person, but we freely chose this state. We are not free to have intimate sexual relations with others (which would be sin), but we chose to be in this state. No one forced us there. Likewise, without a prior state of the freedom to sin we could not properly and satisfactorily reach the higher state of the freedom from sin.

So lower-level freedom (in this world) involves the freedom to sin—the power of contrary choice. In heaven, we trade in this lower freedom for a higher freedom, the way one who is dating trades in the ability to choose many life-partners for the joy and fulfillment of having only one—the one to which we are bound in love (by our free choice) until death.

It would be wrong to claim that we are not free in marriage simply because we should not date or mate with anyone else. Our freedom was expressed at the marriage ceremony when we freely promised to "forsake all others" and cling only to our spouse. Thus we did not really lose true freedom in marriage; rather, we gained a higher freedom that is fulfilled in the bonds of marriage, which we freely chose.

In like manner, when we pass though the veil between this life and the next one, we do not really lose freedom but gain a higher freedom. True, we no longer are free to sin, but that is hardly a loss; rather it is a great gain. To be sure, we no longer have the lower-level freedom to do evil; it is replaced by a higher freedom from all evil.

As to why God could not make this ultimate condition of being freed from all sin up front: Heaven is the end, and earth is the means. One cannot get to the Promised Land without going though the wilderness. Earth is the testing ground; heaven is our final home. We cannot reach home without the proving grounds.

Allowing the choice of good or evil is necessary in achieving the highest good. Again, the highest freedom is *from* sin (heaven), not *of* sin (on earth). One is not fit for the freedom from sin unless he has exercised the freedom to sin, for unless he has had the choice of good over evil, he is not ready for a place where good dominates and evil is defeated. Our initial freedom is designed to lead to the ultimate freedom.

A Free World Where No One Will Sin Is Not a Morally Better World

Granted, it is not possible to have a world where human beings are free but *cannot* sin; nonetheless, there seems to be no contradiction in affirming that they can be free and *will not* sin. After all, Adam was this way before the fall, and Jesus was sinless during His life on earth.

In response, one is tempted simply to say that we are not like Adam before the fall; we are like him after the fall. And we are not Jesus! But there is more that must be said.

The basic point that this view fails to note is that not everything *logically conceivable* is also *actually achievable*. A world of free creatures who never choose to sin is logically possible, for there is no logical contradiction in the basic premise. However, it may be that God in His infinite foreknowledge foresaw that no such world would actually materialize. That is, He knew in advance when He created this world that no such world as one with free creatures, all of whom would never sin, would actually come into being. In other words, He foresaw that every world of free creatures He could ever make would have some who would freely choose to sin. So while such a world is *conceivable*, God knew it was *unachievable*.

Indeed, if everyone were really free to sin but no one ever sinned, then one would suspect that the "dice" of freedom were loaded in one direction. Certainly if on the flip of every coin it always came up heads, we could easily conclude the coin is loaded.

Furthermore, even if such a world could exist, it is still possible that such a world would not be the best possible world. The best possible world would be one where people were truly free to sin, did sin, but despite their sin God brought about a greater good by allowing it and then providing satisfaction and forgiveness for it. Only in this kind of world can the higher virtues be attained. Consider the following:

1. God is the best of all possible beings.
2. If the best of all beings decides to create, then He must create the best of all possible worlds (though He also is free not to create).
3. The best of all possible worlds is one where the higher virtues are attained and sin is defeated, for there is
   a. No courage without danger
   b. No patience without tribulation
   c. No gain without pain
   d. No character without adversity
   e. No forgiveness without sin.
4. Sin cannot be defeated and higher virtues attained, if sin does not actually occur.
5. Hence a world where sin never occurs would not be the best possible world.

In short, even if a free but sinless world is actually achievable, it may be morally less desirable, since the greatest good would not be achieved in it. At the same time, this world may not be the best world possible, but it may be the best *way* possible to the best possible world achievable: Permitting sin to defeat sin and to achieve greater virtues is morally superior to a sinless free world where this greater good is never accomplished.

At this point the objector may back off and ask why God has to produce the best world possible. Why can't He just produce a good world? But this path is fatal to the anti-theist's cause, because either God must produce the best world possible in the end, or He does not have to do so. If He does not, then one cannot object to this world on the grounds that there are better worlds; it is a good one, and good ones are sufficient for God to produce. If, on the other hand, God must produce the best world He can (if He chooses to make one), then a world where sin is tried and defeated and the higher virtues achieved is better than one where they are not. Hence choosing this world as the best way to the best world is the best alternative God could have chosen.

A Free World Where All Would Be Saved May Not Be Actually Achievable

One may respond "Well and good" to the points just made—provided that everyone learns the lessons and all are eventually saved. But according to the Bible and traditional Christianity, this is not the case. Hell exists, and there will be many people in it (see chapter 9). Surely with this greater loss of human souls one could not call ours the greatest world possible.

Again, in response, the same point must be made. A world with even one person in hell would not be the best world *conceivable.* But granting that creatures are truly free, a world with an untold number of people in hell may be the best world *achievable.* This is because not everything logically possible is actually attainable. For example, it is logically possible that more people could have voted for another candidate in the last election, but it is not actually achievable because they chose to vote for the other candidate. In the same way, it is possible that the amount of people in heaven, even though it is less than all persons who ever lived, is the highest number of people God knew He could achieve getting there without violating their free choice.

Forcing people to "freely" believe is a contradiction in terms. God is love (1 John 4:16), and love cannot work coercively— only persuasively. As the philosopher Alvin Plantinga argued, "fettered" freedom is not really freedom (*God, Freedom and Evil*), and as many a young man has discovered, no matter how persuasive one is, the other person is always free to refuse your marriage proposal. That's the way it is in a free world.

Even Jesus was not able to persuade all His people to believe (Matthew 23:37). C. S. Lewis said, "There are only two kinds of people in the end: those who say to God, 'Thy will be done,' and those to whom God says, in the end, '*Thy* will be done.' All that are in Hell, chose it. Without that self-choice there could be no Hell" (*The Great Divorce*, 69).

THE PROBLEM WITH UNIVERSALISM

Of course God wants everyone to be saved. "God so loved the world [not just select individuals] that He gave His one and only Son" (John 3:16). And "He is the propitiation for our sins, and not for ours only but also for the sins of the whole world" (1 John 2:2 ESV). Indeed, "God our Savior . . . desires all people to be saved and to come to the knowledge of the truth" (1 Timothy 2:3–4 ESV), for "The Lord is . . . patient with you, not wanting anyone to perish, but everyone to come to repentance" (2 Peter 3:9).

The problem is that all do not want to be saved. That is to say, God is willing to save all, but all are not willing to be saved (Lewis, *The Problem of Pain*, 106–107).

In Milton's *Paradise Lost,* Satan said: "Better to reign in Hell than serve in Heaven." However, those who follow Satan will hear God reluctantly and sadly say to them on that final day, "Have it as you will." A better world than this one—where all are not saved—*is* conceivable. But unfortunately it is not achievable, because some will not to be saved.

The nature of an all-good God assures us that this world, which He did create, is the best one achievable without violating anyone's free will. As has been shown, no other world is morally superior to this one in which all moral agents are free, where sin is permitted, where sin is defeated, and where the greater virtues are attained by the maximum number of people. All other worlds are not moral, not possible, not achievable with free creatures, and/or morally inferior. *This present world is not the best of all possible worlds, but it is the best of all possible ways to the best of all achievable worlds.*

So if God knew this world would be as evil as it is, then why did He choose to make it? Because He is the best of all beings possible and, as such, He must produce the best of all worlds actually possible (if He is going to create). Permitting this evil world is the best of all possible ways to produce the best of all possible worlds. Our own societies are an illustration of this point. We permit cars, boats, and airplanes knowing there will be accidents and deaths. Nonetheless, we deem that the end of human freedom, mobility, and happiness justifies permitting (though discouraging) the evils we know will sometimes happen. God does the same with His world.

As for the objection that God is employing an illegitimate "end justifies the means" ethic, we note a crucial difference. God is not *producing* or *promoting* evil means to attain a good end. He is *permitting* them. A good parent permits a possible accident every time he permits his teenager to drive the family car; however, he is not promoting it. Likewise, no reasonable person beats his head on a wall because it feels so good when he stops; however, one does permit the pain of the dentist chair in order to produce the good results. *God allows evil to produce the greater good.*

The Problem of Physical Evil

When it comes to pain, most of us are chickens. We'd do almost anything to avoid it. Even a little needle prick in the doctor's office is frightening to many. We take pain pills, sleeping pills, and sedatives. Pain avoidance is an occupational hazard for most Americans. We go to great pains to avoid pain. We even have amnesia sedatives now that erase all memory of painful procedures.

All pain is not physical. My wife would rather make three right turns than face the pain of one left turn against traffic. Her memory of the pain of being hit on two occasions while making left turns is enough to prompt her to go to the trouble of making three times as many turns to get to her destination.

Of course, when we speak of the problem of pain, we are speaking of much greater pain than relatively trivial examples. Critics sometimes speak of "the sum total of human pain"— and it is a huge sum. This is a diversion of the issue, since no single individual has ever experienced "the sum total of human pain." Indeed, no one ever experienced a lifetime of pain; they only experience the present moment of pain—even if these moments continue to come for a long time. Nonetheless, in many respects physical evil is the most pressing of evil's problems.

Physical evil, suffering, and pain are where the rubber meets the road. Other aspects of the problem are intellectually tough, but this dimension is experientially tough through and through. The title of a good book on the topic by Philip Yancey says it well: *Where Is God When It Hurts?* C. S. Lewis put a lot of *thought* into his classic treatment of *The Problem of Pain*. But when his wife died, he put a lot of *feeling* into *A Grief Observed*. The first book was a matter of the *mind*; the latter was a matter of the *heart*. Evil and suffering become a lot more real when it hits close to home. Every pastor knows the death of a friend or relative is a lot harder than the funeral of a stranger.

THE PROBLEM OF PHYSICAL EVIL

The solution to the problem of moral evil offered above (chapters 3 through 5) is based on free will. Evil makes sense only in that context. There is no real problem of evil in an unreal world of robots or puppets. Grief is for real people.

However, the problem of evil is real for human beings, and the problem of physical evil is acutely real. The reason for this is that while moral evil can be explained by free choice, it is not apparent how all physical evil can be explained this way. It seems obvious to most that no natural disaster was created by our free choice. No one wills a lightning strike or a tsunami on themselves. The argument can be stated as follows:

1. Moral evil is explained by free will.
2. But much of physical evil does not result from our

free will (e.g., floods, genetic deformity, cancer, and death).

3. Therefore, much of physical evil cannot be explained by free choice.

4. Hence either God or nature (which He created) must be the cause of these physical evils.

5. But both of these are traceable to God and are His responsibility.

6. Such evils are incompatible with an all-loving, all-powerful God.

7. Therefore, a theistic God does not exist.

The finite godist John Stuart Mill gave a poignant focus to the problem:

> In sober truth, nearly all the things which men are hanged or imprisoned for doing are nature's everyday performances. Killing, the most criminal act recognized by human laws, nature does once to every being that lives, and in a large proportion of cases after protracted tortures such as only the greatest monsters . . . inflict on their living fellow creatures. (*Nature and Utility of Religion*, 28–29)

RESPONSE TO THE PROBLEM OF PHYSICAL EVIL

In reply, the theist can argue that all physical evil is connected to free will. Some is connected directly, some indirectly. Most is connected with human free will, though some may be connected to free actions of evil spirits (demons). But all physical evil is connected with free moral agents in one way or another.

1. Some Physical Evil Is Directly Self-Inflicted.

Much physical suffering results directly from misuse of our own bodies. Smoking, alcohol, and other drug use cause untold physical harm and death. Overeating and other bad eating habits are also responsible for a significant percentage of sickness and death. Lack of proper exercise also causes many physical problems. We can hardly blame God for things we inflict on ourselves. Some medical sources have argued that most major illnesses are the result of a failure of human beings to follow basic guidelines of health and sanitation set down in the Bible (see *None of These Diseases* by S. I. McMillen).

2. Some Physical Evil Is an Indirect Result of Free Choice.

The effects of some free choices are indirect. Some self-inflicted physical conditions are the result of our free choices. For example, the choice to be lazy can result in poverty (Proverbs 24:33–34). Many children have died of neglect, being left home alone or in places without adult supervision. Deserts and dust bowls have been known to result from improper cultivation practices. For instance, overgrazing can cause arid conditions.

3. Some Physical Evil Is the Direct Result of the Free Choices of Others.

Child and spousal abuse does not result from divine action—they're direct results of the bad choices and actions of other persons. This is to say nothing of injust war, cruelty, and torture. We can hardly blame God for these actions. The truth is that in a free world the result of one person's freedom impinges on another person's life. Drunk drivers often kill other people. Cell phones are a blessing, but they also cause accidents in which others are injured or killed.

4. Some Physical Evil Is the Indirect Result of the Free Choices of Others.

Some persons make non-malicious choices that affect others indirectly. Thoughtless choices resulting in poverty can cause starvation or malnourishment of dependents. As we have seen in the recent recession, greed can cause the loss of jobs and poverty for others. Much of world poverty is caused by the siphoning of gifts and goods intended for the poor. Once again, this cannot be laid at the doorstep of the divine. Professor Cal Beisner has demonstrated this point well in his books *Man, Economy, and Environment in Biblical Perspective; Prospects for Growth: A Biblical View of Population Resources and the Future*; and *Prosperity and Poverty: The Compassionate Use of Resources in a World of Scarcity*.

5. Some Physical Evil Is the Byproduct of a Good Process.

Drowning is a byproduct of having water at our disposal to enjoy. Unintentional shooting deaths occur with guns meant for sport or food gathering. Rain that nourishes the soil also causes floods. Winds renew the air, but tornados sometimes spin up. Earthquakes recycle minerals needed for life but also cause death and destruction. Both hurricanes and tsunamis are byproducts of good natural processes. The greater enjoyment of flying, boating, or mountain climbing are the occasion of accidents that are byproducts of a good practice. Every step is a potential fall, but no one would insist we shouldn't learn to walk.

6. Some Physical Evil Is Necessary for the Greater Physical Good.

The early bird gets the worm, but the worm gets eaten. Higher forms of life feed off of lower forms. The greater good is sustained by the consumption of lower forms of life. Since no moral creature is consumed, there is no moral problem here.[1] Much physical evil can be explained as necessary to achieve a greater physical good.

7. Some Physical Evil Is Needed for a Greater Moral Good.

We have seen that C. S. Lewis identified another purpose for allowing physical evils: "God whispers to us in our pleasures, speaks in our conscience, but shouts in our pain: it is his megaphone to rouse a deaf world" (*Problem of Pain*, 81). The truth is that we learn more enduring lessons in life through pain than through pleasure. Once more, since God is a moral being who made us moral beings like Himself and wants us to be morally perfect like Himself (Matthew 5:48), it is understandable that He would be more interested in our character than our comfort; more concerned about our holiness than our happiness (e.g., see Romans 5:3–4; James 1:2–4; 2 Corinthians 4:17; Hebrews 12:11).

8. Some Physical Evil May Be Inflicted by God's Justice in Punishing Evil Actions.

Most physical evils in the world can be explained, as above, by human free choices directly or indirectly. There are, however,

---

[1] This is not to say that animal cruelty is not a moral problem. It is morally wrong to be cruel to animals (see *Christian Ethics*, chapter 19). It is only to say that animals are not moral beings. They are not made in the image of God as humans are (Genesis 1:27; 9:6). Hence it is not murder to take their lives to sustain ours.

some physical events that result from God's judgment. According to the Bible, God sometimes has used physical calamities, like plagues (Exodus 7–11), famines (Isaiah 14:30), sicknesses (2 Kings 20), and death (Roman 5:12; 1 Corinthians 11:28–30).

9. *Some Physical Evil Is a Result of Adam's Free Choice.*

According to the Bible, much physical evil, including sickness and death, has resulted from Adam's sin: "Just as sin entered the world through one man, and death through sin, and in this way death came to all men because all sinned [in Adam]—for before the law was given, sin was in the world" (Romans 5:12). This occurred in Genesis where God warned Adam, "You are free to eat from any tree in the garden; but you must not eat from the tree of the knowledge of good and evil, for when you eat of it you will surely die" (Genesis 2:16–17). When they disobeyed, God said to Eve, "I will greatly increase your pains in childbearing; with pain you will give birth to children" (3:16). To Adam he added,

> Because you have listened to the voice of your wife, and have eaten from the tree about which I commanded you, saying, "You shall not eat from it"; Cursed is the ground because of you; in toil you will eat of it all the days of your life. Both thorns and thistles it shall grow for you; and you will eat the plants of the field; by the sweat of your face you will eat bread, till you return to the ground, because from it you were taken; for you are dust, and to dust you shall return. (3:17–19 NASB)

Paul said,

> The creation was subjected to futility, not willingly, but because of Him who subjected it, in hope that the creation itself also will be set free from its slavery to corruption into the freedom

of the glory of the children of God. For we know that the whole creation groans and suffers the pains of childbirth together until now. (Romans 8:20–22 NASB)

If this is taken to mean that all physical evils (except direct divine judgments) are a result of the fall, then it would trace all physical evil back to the sin of Adam. On this view, no other explanation is needed to account for physical calamities, sickness, and death. Connected with a young-earth view of creation, this is taken to account for all death, including animal death by carnivorous animals; the fossil remains are a result of the flood and did not exist before Adam. Others who hold an old-earth view believe either that only human death, not animal death, resulted from Adam's fall or else that the death of animals before Adam during the geological ages was anticipatory of the fall (see appendix 1). In either event, physical evil in the created world is related to free choices of human beings.

10. Some Physical Evil Is a Result of Evil Spirit Beings.

The Bible also speaks about evil resulting from the work of evil spiritual creatures. God created only good creatures (Genesis 1:31; 1 Timothy 4:4), but some of them, led by Lucifer, an archangel (who became Satan), rebelled against God (Revelation 12:4) and became evil spirits or demons. According to the Bible, these evil spirits are opposed to God and God's people and wish to destroy them. The Gospels attribute some sickness and suffering to demon possession (Matthew 9:32–33; 8:16; 15:22). According to Job, Satan was permitted by God to inflict disaster and death on him and his family (Job 1). Some have suggested that these spirits could be behind the other physical evils not attributable to human free choices (e.g., see Alvin Plantinga, *God, Freedom, and Evil*).

WHY GOD DOES NOT MIRACULOUSLY INTERVENE

Some have objected to claiming that physical evil results from the abuse of free will, insisting that God could miraculously intervene and prevent these evil results; that He does not makes God culpable for allowing them to occur. However, as we later show in more detail (see chapter 8), regular miraculous intervention for this purpose would upset the whole world's moral order. Without the regularity of nature, moral decisions are impossible and moral improvement cannot occur; both of these are necessary to producing the best of all worlds.

CAMUS'S CONUNDRUM

The French existential atheist Albert Camus posed a conundrum for the Christian view of physical evil. In *The Plague*, he argued that if physical evil is a result of God's judgment, then a dilemma follows for the Christian:

1. Either one joins the doctor and fights the plague, or else he joins the priest and does not fight the plague.
2. But not to fight the plague is anti-humanitarian.
3. And to fight the plague is to fight against God who sent it.
4. Therefore, if humanitarianism is right, then theism is wrong.

The Christian response is to deny premise 3. First, the plague (physical evil in the world) in the general and universal sense is the result of the fall of humankind. The fall resulted from man's sin, so to fight the plague is not to fight against God but against sin and thus to be on God's side. One need not be "anti-humanitarian" to fight sin; indeed, one is pro-Christian, because fighting the fall is what Christianity is all about. In biblical terms this is called redemption (Romans 3:23–24).

Second, "joining the doctor" is not humanitarianism, it is Christian, for only the Great Physician (Christ) can save. Only Christ can cure sin (Hebrews 1:3; 9:22; 10:14). A humanitarian effort can at best treat the symptoms, not the disease. Jesus said, "I am the way and the truth and the life. No one comes to the Father except through me" (John 14:6). Paul added, "There is one God and one mediator between God and men, the man Christ Jesus" (1 Timothy 2:5).

So the dilemma for Camus and the non-Christian view is this:

1. Everyone should fight the plague.
2. Either we fight the plague effectively or ineffectively.
3. To fight the plague effectively we must treat the disease, not just the symptoms.
4. Only Christ has treated the disease of sin itself and provided a cure (salvation: Mark 10:33–34; Acts 13:38–39; Colossians 2:14–15).
5. Only those who follow Christ's way of salvation (Acts 16:31; Romans 10:9) are effectively fighting the plague.
6. Other attempts to fight the plague—no matter how "humanitarian" they may be—ultimately will be ineffective. At best, they will be treating symptoms, not helping to cure the disease of sin.

It is charged that much physical evil is not the result of free choices and, therefore, can be blamed on God. But the above discussion shows that all physical evil can be related to free choice, either directly or indirectly. According to one view, Adam's sin alone could account for all physical evils. Add to that the evils inflicted by Satan and evil spirits and one need look no further for the possible explanation of all physical evil.

No doubt God's moral purposes in allowing pain and suffering are revealed through suffering. The bottom line is this: The above explanations combined, or given numbers of them, can account for all physical evil in the universe. There is no reason to either demote God to finite or to deny His existence in order to explain the presence of physical evil.

Chapter 8

Miracles and Evil

One of the objections to the theist's contention that there are physical consequences to free choices is that God could supernaturally prevent these physical consequences. That is, there could be free choices without undesirable physical consequences, if God intervened to prevent them. If this is the case, then the theistic explanations would be ineffective, since God could have prevented all physical evil.

For example, every time a would-be murderer attempted to kill an innocent person, God could intercept the bullet before it hit its victim. Every knife used in an attempted assault could be miraculously turned into jelly. In every attempted choking, the noose could be turned into a noodle. All poison aimed at killing someone could be chemically neutralized, and so on.

If God has supernatural powers, as theists say He has, then these events are not impossible. Only what is actually impossible is beyond supernatural intervention. Hence the objection could be stated this way:

1. If God is all-powerful, He could supernaturally intervene to stop all physical evils.

2. If God is all-good, He would miraculously intervene to stop all physical evils.
3. There is much physical evil God does not intervene to stop.
4. Hence there is no all-powerful and all-loving God.

Let's analyze these premises one by one to see if the conclusion follows.

Premise 1: *If God is all-powerful, He could stop all physical evils.*

As stated, this premise is untrue; there are many things even an all-powerful (omnipotent) being cannot do. Several come to mind.

First, God cannot perform any miracle that involves a logical or actual impossibility. God cannot make 2 plus 2 equal 5. God can't make a logical contradiction into a non-contradiction without changing the premises. Nor could He perform impossible miracles like making a stick with one end. Nor could He make two mountains without a valley.

Second, God can't make an infinitely heavy stone. No matter how big it is, it could always be bigger. There cannot be anything bigger than an infinitely large object; hence every stone He makes is finite. And being infinite in power, He can lift any finite stone.

Third, God cannot make it rain and not rain in the same place at the same time in answer to opposing prayers. Nor could He miraculously intervene to make opposing armies win the same war. In short, omnipotence is limited by what is logically or actually possible. God can only do the possible. Miracles cannot violate the law of non-contradiction. God cannot literally intervene and stop all physical evil; some such interventions would be impossible. So the best one could say is:

Premise 1a: *If God is all-powerful, He could stop all physical evils that are not logically or actually impossible.*

Premise 3: *There is much physical evil God does not intervene to stop.*

We'll examine this briefly before premise 2, and we need not spend much time here. Obviously there are some miracles God could do that He does not do. For example, He could heal more people than He does. Not all prayers for miraculous healings are answered positively. Many good and godly people are seriously ill or handicapped much of their lives, like Joni Eareckson Tada or the apostle Paul (2 Corinthians 12:5–10).

God can raise the dead and did so several times in the Bible (cf. John 11:1–43; Acts 20:7–12). But many sincere and godly people have cried out to God to do the same for their dead loved ones, only to have their request rejected. So there are many more providential and miraculous interventions that God could do but does not do. This leads us to the most problematic statement.

Premise 2: *If God is all-good, He would miraculously intervene to stop all physical evils.*

This premise assumes that God will automatically perform whatever is logically and actually possible to do in preventing physical evils. But this does not follow from His nature as all-loving. Sometimes the most loving thing God can do is not to supernaturally intervene to prevent all physical evil in our lives. By analogy, all good parents know that to give a child everything he/she wants is not the loving thing to do. Sometimes tough love is necessary. Sometimes it's necessary to allow them to learn the hard way. Sometimes it's better to allow them to struggle. And all good parents know that it is destructive to relieve all pain from a child's life. Our heavenly Father knows this infinitely better than we do (Matthew 6:30–34).

To put it another way, there are reasons other than *logical* and *actual* impossibilities for God not to supernaturally intervene in the physical world to prevent all pain, suffering, and evil. There are *moral* reasons. Even the Bible speaks of a time Jesus "could not do any miracles there" (Mark 6:5); clearly this was not a logical or actual "could not" but a moral one, for He did some miracles there. The constraint on Jesus not to perform any other miracles was moral—He was morally constrained not to do it because "he was amazed at their lack of faith" (v. 6). In a parallel passage it says "He *did not* do many miracles there because of their lack of faith" (Matthew 13:58).

The story is told of the Christian confined for life to a wheelchair. Her zealous friends cried out to God on her behalf to no avail. One person cruelly concluded that the disabled person did not have enough faith to be healed and get out of that chair. To which she replied, "*You* do not have enough faith to get *into* this chair!" The truth is that God delivers some people *from* their sickness and others *through* their sickness. Both are the hand of God.

REASONS GOD DOES NOT ALWAYS MIRACULOUSLY PREVENT PHYSICAL EVIL

There are many good reasons why God does not always perform a miracle to avert our pain and suffering. The following list is suggestive, not necessarily exhaustive.

1. *It Is Not Possible to Have a Regular Miraculous Interruption of the Natural Order.*

In order for God to disrupt all physical evils, He would have to do miracles constantly, since physical evils are constantly happening. But a regular interruption of the natural order is impossible; a miracle by definition is an irregular event. And it is contradictory for God to do the irregular regularly. Miracles are only possible on the backdrop of natural law, for if there were no regular way that nature operated, then there could not be any irregular (miraculous) events.

2. *Constant Miracles Would Disrupt the Natural Order Necessary for Physical Life.*

Physical life is not actually possible in a world where miracles happen regularly. All of life as we know it depends on the regularity of nature. We cannot even eat, drink, walk, or talk without depending on the regularity of gravity, inertia, motion, and other laws. If we can't depend on gravity, then we don't know whether ingesting water will take it down our throat or up our nose. We could not cook food, operate a car, or almost anything else we can think of without depending on constant, regular laws uninterrupted by continual miracles.

3. *Constant Miracles Would Hinder the Full Exercise of Moral Freedom.*

Regular miraculous interruption of the physical world would also disrupt the full exercise of our moral freedom. In a free world, such as God has chosen to make, free creatures must be allowed room to express their freedom. If God stopped all free thoughts and actions by not allowing them to materialize, He would be negating the very freedom He granted in making this a free moral world. Surely God has the power to stop all atheists, skeptics, and agnostics from expressing themselves. He could make them mute every time they attempted to say something against Him. But then they would not really be free to express their views. And if a person is not free to speak against God (only for God), then He is not really free to choose what he wills. The same is true of all expressions of evil. Continued miraculous disruption is contrary to the free expression of moral creatures.

4. It Would Disrupt the Natural Order Necessary for Making Rational and Moral Choices.

What is more, rational and moral choices are only possible in a world of regular events. Rational decisions are dependent on knowing that events will unfold regularly. Unless we can predict the future (based on past regularity), we will not know what acts would be harmful and what would be helpful. For instance, unless we know bullets will perform the same devastating way when pointed at a target as they did in practice, we would not have a rational basis for knowing they can be fatal when shot at other humans. This is why we do not hold little children culpable for injuries and deaths resulting from playing with dangerous things.

So morality follows upon rationality, and rationality is dependent on regularity.

This is true in all of life. Unless we know based on past regularity that the laws of nature will behave the same way today as they did yesterday, the very basis for rational and morally responsible decisions is destroyed. Constant miraculous interruption of the natural order would destroy the very order necessary for making moral decisions.

5. *Constant Miracles Would Defeat the Conditions for Moral Improvement.*

In the physical world, physical consequences for actions are necessary for learning which actions are good and which are bad. If we get pleasure from one action and pain from another, we tend to do the one and avoid the other. Physical reward and punishment are necessary to learn which choices are good and which are not. But if God constantly intervened to save us from bad consequences by bad actions, He would be eliminating a significant element in learning moral lessons. As we learned earlier (in chapter 7), pain is an effective way to keep us from self-destruction.

6. *Constant Miraculous Intervention Would Hinder One of God's Most Effective Ways of Providing Moral Warnings.*

Few enduring moral lessons are learned through pleasure; most are learned through pain. This being the case, miraculous intervention to eliminate all painful consequences of actions would eliminate lessons on moral improvement to be learned through them.

By miraculously removing all physical discomfort, God would not only be working against Himself but against us. Moral exhortation is crucial in moral improvement. Thus, eliminating one of the best sources of moral exhortation would be eliminating one of the best means of moral improvement.

7. *Continued Miraculous Intervention Would Eliminate an Important Precondition for Achieving the Best World Possible.*

As we have seen (in chapter 6), this is not the best world possible, but it is the best way to the best world achievable. A world of pain, danger, and sin is a necessary condition for attaining a world without any of these preconditions. No pain, no gain. Without danger, the virtue of courage cannot be developed. Without trials and tribulations we can have no patience. God has to permit sin before we can experience forgiveness. Higher-order virtues are dependent on allowing lower-order evils.

By miraculously eliminating physical evils (of pain and suffering), such as we have, God would be eliminating the very means necessary for achieving the best world possible. As the best Being possible, God must do the best thing possible. Hence, God must allow (and not miraculously disrupt) the very means necessary for producing the best world possible.

Some have suggested that "omnipotence could have created creatures who he could have been sure would respond to the appropriate challenge by a willing exercise of fortitude, without these creatures having to acquire this character by any actual exercise of fortitude" (John Hick, "Divine Omnipotence and Human Freedom" in *New Essays in Philosophical Theology*, 155). However, there are several problems with this view.

First, no real evidence is shown as to how such persons are more than hypothetically possible (i.e., actually possible).

Second, there seems to be some confusion here with what is logically possible (i.e., involves no logical contradiction) and what is actually achievable. Actual experience is to the contrary.

Third, of course God could program good behavior into creatures, but then it would not really be virtuous behavior since they could not help being that way. The truth is that higher virtues can only be attained by free beings that have struggled with evil and been victorious over it.

Desirable behavior is not necessarily the result of character. There are animals with good temperaments. We can program robots to react in desirable ways, but this is not virtue.

Of course, not all persons will achieve the higher virtues and the greater good possible. Some sufferers get better, and some get bitter. For some it is a stumbling stone, for others a stepping stone. Indeed, even though all people have the opportunity for heaven, nonetheless, some will end in hell (see chapter 9). In a free world, not all will freely choose the good; some will choose evil.

One thing is certain: Given that we are free moral creatures, even an all-powerful God will not persuade all to choose the right way. As an all-loving Being, He cannot work coercively but only persuasively. Love never forces itself on another's will. So in a free universe, we will not end with the best world conceivable but with the best world achievable by God's grace in coordination with our free will (see C. S. Lewis, *The Great Divorce*, 69).

WHY GOD DOES NOT MIRACULOUSLY INTERVENE MORE OFTEN

Granting the need for physical evil to make rational and moral actions possible in our world, and granting it is necessary to achieve the best world possible, there are still some questions to answer. First, why does not God intervene more often than He does? Did He have to allow all of this evil in order to accomplish His purposes? And did He have to take this long to do it? One feels the need to cry out with the prophet: "How long will the land mourn?" (Jeremiah 12:4 NKJV). Would it disrupt some great eternal plan if God allowed less evil and intervened more often?

Of course the answers to how long and how much physical pain and suffering would be necessary to accomplish God's purposes are known only to God. After all, He alone is all-knowing, and we by comparison to His infinite mind are almost totally ignorant. One thing is certain: A pint-sized human brain is in no position to dictate to the Omniscient One what is too much or too long! (Deuteronomy 29:29; Romans 11:33). Of this we can be sure, based on the fact that God is both all-good and all-knowing: It won't be too long, and it won't be too much.

Further, based on the fact that God is all-powerful, we can know that whatever evil He permits and whatever time He allows, He will be victorious in the end. After all, the worst enemy is not suffering, but death, and that will be defeated: "He must reign until he has put all his enemies under his feet. The last enemy to be destroyed is death" (1 Corinthians 15:25–26). Viewing it in the light of eternity, we can say with the apostle, "This light momentary affliction is preparing for us an eternal weight of glory beyond all comparison" (2 Corinthians 4:17 ESV).

WHY GOD DIDN'T MAKE US A PURE SPIRIT WITH NO BODY (AND BODILY PAIN)

Of course, one could always ask why we need bodies. If we were pure spirits, then we could not suffer all this physical pain. The answer is twofold.

First, God did make pure spirits; they are called angels. But they too sinned, and they too suffer pain (Matthew 8:28–29; Revelation 20:10). Not all pain is physical.

Second, we have a seeming redemptive advantage over angels. Once angels sinned, they were doomed forever with no possibility of salvation: "God did not spare angels when they sinned, but sent them to hell" (2 Peter 2:4). Christ did not die for angels:

> Since therefore the children share in flesh and blood, he himself likewise partook of the same things, that through death he might destroy the one who has the power of death, that is, the devil, and deliver all those who through fear of death were subject to lifelong slavery. For surely it is not angels that he helps, but he helps the offspring of Abraham. (Hebrews 2:14–16 ESV)

Indeed, when fallen angels are mentioned in the Bible it is in connection with their condemnation (cf. Matthew 8:29; 2 Peter 2:4; Jude 6–7; Revelation 12:3–10). Through the cross, "He disarmed the [spiritual] rulers and authorities and put them to open shame, by triumphing over them" (Colossians 2:15 ESV).

The reason that angels, once they sin, are eternally condemned and not savable is that, unlike humans, they have no bodies of their own (though some have assumed bodily form on occasion—Genesis 18). Angels have no children (Matthew 22:30). They never grow up or grow old. They do not undergo change. They are all pure spirits (Hebrews 1:14; Luke 24:39). It is living in a changing body that makes change possible for humans—and redemption is a change.

Once an angel decides against God (Revelation 12:3–4), its decision can never be changed. Their minds are set forever. Once they made the choice to reject God, it was as final as a human's final choice is at the moment of death (Hebrews 9:27). This is why the Bible never calls upon them to repent, as it does people (Acts 17:30). Thus Anselm noted, "As they fell with none to plot their fall, so they must rise with none to aid them" (Anselm, *Cur Deus Homo*, 2.21). They had no tempter but fell by a sheer act of pride (1 Timothy 3:6). Since they could not be tempted to sin, neither can they be wooed into redemption. Once made up, their mind is fixed forever.

To be sure, angels, unlike human beings, cannot suffer physical pain or death (Luke 20:34–36). But, unlike humans, neither can angels experience physical pleasures like touching a baby's skin, eating a juicy steak, or enjoying sexual intimacy. In short, God can and did make pure spirits, unchangeable in their nature. They are called angels, and they cannot be redeemed. On the contrary, human beings can change and hence can go through the changing process of redemption.

To summarize, the argument from miracles against the theistic solution to physical evil falls short of its goal. It contends that:

1. If God is all-powerful, He could supernaturally intervene to stop all physical evils.
2. If God is all-good, He would miraculously intervene to stop physical evils.
3. There is much physical evil God does not intervene to stop.
4. Hence there is no all-powerful and all-loving God.

However, the first premise has serious qualifications since even an all-powerful being cannot literally do anything—for example, perform miracles that are logically contradictory or actually impossible.

Furthermore, the second premise clearly is false, since it assumes that God will do things against His moral best judgment to do what achieves the best possible world. And this would eliminate the very physical conditions that make moral freedom possible and the greater moral good achievable. Therefore, the argument for miraculous intervention to alleviate all physical evils fails. As for whether God supernaturally or providentially has intervened to stop some physical evils, the answer is yes, and there are numerous examples inside and outside the Bible to demonstrate that He has. As to why He does not do it more, only an infinite Mind knows exactly how much is enough.

Chapter 9

The Problem of Eternal Evil (Hell)

We have another issue. Even granting the above solutions to the various problems of evil (chapters 1 through 7), historic Christianity of all major branches holds to the doctrine of eternal punishment for the wicked. The Athanasian Creed declares:

> From thence [Heaven] He shall come to judge the quick [alive] and the dead. At whose coming all men shall rise again with their bodies; and shall give account of their own works. And they that have done good shall go into life everlasting and *they that have done evil into everlasting fire*. (no. 43)

Few doctrines have been attacked more than the doctrine of eternal conscious punishment. Unbelievers generally question both hell's existence and justice; they also have called hell cruel and barbarous. Bertrand Russell said anyone who threatens people with eternal punishment, as Jesus did, is inhumane ("Why I Am Not a Christian" in *The Writings of Bertrand Russell*, 593–594). Orthodox Christians, both Catholic and Protestant, have defended both hell's reality and equity.

THE PROBLEM OF ETERNAL EVIL

There are numerous objections to eternal punishment; each will be stated and then evaluated. First, if God is all-loving, then why punish people at all—why not just rehabilitate them? Second, even if punishment is justified, why punish them forever—isn't this gigantic overkill? Why not have a temporary hell (or purgatory), followed by an eternal heaven, after the wicked are punished temporally? Third, why have a hell at all—why not just annihilate them? Fourth, why not just save everyone?

These are four "category alternatives" to hell: rehabilitationism, purgationism, annihilationism, and universalism. Evidence for the orthodox doctrine of hell—that is, an eternal conscious state for the wicked—argues against all four.

EVIDENCE FOR THE EXISTENCE OF HELL

The evidence for hell is biblical, rational, and moral. Perhaps the strongest of all arguments is that Jesus Christ, whom orthodox Christians believe is God, affirmed hell's existence. Indeed, He had more to say about hell than heaven.

Jesus Affirmed the Existence of Hell

Jesus warned, "Do not be afraid of those who kill the body but cannot kill the soul. Rather, be afraid of the One who can destroy both soul and body in hell" (Matthew 10:28). He added of those who reject Him, "As the weeds are pulled up and burned in the fire, so it will be at the end of the age" (13:40). In His Mount Olivet Discourse, the Lord declared, "Then he will say to those on his left, 'Depart from me, you who are cursed, into the eternal fire prepared for the devil and his angels' " (25:41).

Elsewhere Jesus affirmed: "If your hand causes you to sin, cut it off. It is better for you to enter life maimed than with two hands to go into hell, where the fire never goes out" (Mark 9:43). The reality of hell is obvious from a vivid story told by Jesus in Luke 16. This story is unlike a parable, since in it Jesus uses the actual name of a person.

> There was a rich man who was dressed in purple and fine linen and lived in luxury every day. At his gate was laid a beggar named Lazarus . . . the beggar died and the angels carried him to Abraham's side. The rich man also died and was buried. In hell, where he was in torment, he looked up and saw Abraham far away, with Lazarus by his side. So he called to him, "Father Abraham, have pity on me and send Lazarus to dip the tip of his finger in water and cool my tongue, because I am in agony in this fire." But Abraham replied, "Son, remember that in your lifetime you received your good things, while Lazarus received bad things, but now he is comforted here and you are in agony. And besides all this, between us and you a great chasm has been fixed, so that those who want to go from here to you cannot, nor can anyone cross over from there to us." He answered, "Then I beg you, father, send Lazarus to my father's house, for I have five brothers. Let him warn them, so that they will not also come to this place of torment." Abraham replied, "They have Moses and the Prophets; let them listen to them." "No, father Abraham," he said, "but if someone from the dead goes to them, they will repent." He said to him, "If they do not listen to Moses and the Prophets, they will not be convinced even if someone rises from the dead" (vv. 19–31).

Hell is a place of eternal conscious torment. There is a "great gulf" between it and heaven, which is a place of eternal conscious bliss.

The Bible Affirms There Is a Hell

In addition, the other inspired New Testament writings affirm hell's existence. Perhaps the most gripping of all is found in the last book of the Bible. John declared:

> Then I saw a great white throne and him who was seated on it. Earth and sky fled from his presence, and there was no place for them. And I saw the dead, great and small, standing before the throne, and books were opened. Another book was opened, which is the book of life. The dead were judged according to what they had done as recorded in the books. The sea gave up the dead that were in it, and death and Hades gave up the dead that were in them, and each person was judged according to what he had done. Then death and Hades were thrown into the lake of fire. The lake of fire is the second death. If anyone's name was not found written in the book of life, he was thrown into the lake of fire. (Revelation 20:11–15)

The apostle Paul spoke of everlasting separation from God, saying:

> This will happen when the Lord Jesus is revealed from heaven in blazing fire with his powerful angels. He will punish those who do not know God and do not obey the gospel of our Lord Jesus. They will be punished with everlasting destruction and shut out from the presence of the Lord and from the majesty of his power. (2 Thessalonians 1:7–9)

The writer of Hebrews added a note of finality when he wrote, "Man is destined to die once, and after that to face judgment" (9:27).

God's Justice Demands a Hell

In addition to Scripture's direct affirmations, there are many other reasons for hell's existence. One is that justice demands hell, and God is just (Romans 2). He is so pure and untainted that He cannot even look upon evil (Habakkuk 1:13), and He is no respecter of persons, "for God does not show favoritism" (Romans 2:11). Abraham declared, "Will not the Judge of all the earth do right?" (Genesis 18:25).

But it is a simple fact that not all evil is punished in this life. Many observers have noted that the wicked sometimes prosper (Psalm 73:3). Thus a place of punishment for the wicked after this life is necessary to maintain God's justice.

The early American thinker Jonathan Edwards argued that even one sin deserves hell, since the eternal holy God cannot tolerate any sin. How much more, then, does a multitude of daily sins in thought, word, and deed? This is all compounded by our rejection of God's immense mercy. And add to this man's readiness to find fault with God's justice and mercy, and we have abundant evidence of the need for hell. Thus, Edwards insisted, if we had a true spiritual awareness, we would not be amazed at hell's severity but at our own depravity (*The Works of Jonathan Edwards,* 1.109).

God's Love Demands a Hell

The Bible asserts that "God is love" (1 John 4:16), and again, love cannot act coercively, only persuasively. A God of love cannot force people to love Him. Paul spoke of things being done freely and not of compulsion (2 Corinthians 9:7). C. S. Lewis observed, "the Irresistible and the Indisputable are the two weapons which the very nature of His scheme forbids Him to use. Merely to override a human will . . . would be for Him useless. He cannot ravish. He can only woo" (*The Screwtape Letters,* 46). Those who do not wish to love God must be allowed not to love Him. Those who do not will to be with Him must be allowed to be separated. Hell is eternal separation from God.

Human Dignity Demands a Hell

Since God cannot force people into heaven against their free choice, human free choice demands a hell. Once more, Jesus cried out, "O Jerusalem, Jerusalem, you who kill the prophets and stone those sent to you, how often I have longed to gather your children together, as a hen gathers her chicks under her wings, but *you were not willing*" (Matthew 23:37). And, as Lewis said, "There are only two kinds of people in the end: those who say to God, 'thy will be done,' and those to whom God says, in the end, '*Thy* will be done' " (*The Great Divorce*, 69).

God's Sovereignty Demands a Hell

God is in complete control over the whole universe (see my *Chosen but Free*, chapter 1). Nothing can thwart God's purposes (Job 42:2). God guarantees, in advance, ultimate victory over evil (Revelation 21–22). However, unless there is a hell, there is no final victory over evil, for what frustrates good is evil. The wheat and tares cannot grow together forever (Matthew 13:30 NKJV). The sheep and the goats must be finally separated (25:32). Just like in society, where punishment for evil is necessary that good might prevail, even so in eternity good must triumph over evil. If it does not, then God is not in ultimate control. In brief, God's sovereignty demands a hell, otherwise He would not be the ultimate victor over evil (cf. 1 Corinthians 15:24–28; Revelation 20–22).

The Cross of Christ Implies Hell

At the center of Christianity is the cross (1 Corinthians 1:17–18; 15:3), without which there is no salvation (Romans 4:25; Hebrews 10:10–14). It is the very purpose for which Christ came into the world (Luke 19:10; Mark 10:45), for without the cross no one can be saved (Acts 4:12; John 10:1, 9–10). Only through the cross can we be delivered from our sins (Romans 3:21–26). Jesus suffered great agony and even separation from God (Hebrews 2:10–18; 5:7–9); anticipating the cross, Jesus sweated "as it were great drops of blood" (Luke 22:44 KJV).

But why the cross and all this suffering unless there is a hell? If there is no hell to shun, then the cross is a sham. If there is no hell, only a final nothingness, then Christ literally died to save us from nothing. In this case, Christ's death is robbed of its eternal significance. Unless there is an eternal separation from God from which people need to be delivered, the cross is emptied of its real meaning.

THE REASONABLENESS OF HELL

While many believe hell is unreasonable, the evidence indicates another conclusion. Jonathan Edwards argued for the rationality of hell, saying:

> It is a most unreasonable thing to suppose that there should be no future punishment, to suppose that God, who had made man a rational creature, able to know his duty, and sensible that he is deserving punishment when he does it not; should let man alone, and let him live as he will, and never punish him for his sins, and never make any difference between the good and the bad. . . . How unreasonable it is to suppose, that he who made the world, should leave things in such confusion, and never take any care of

the governing of his creatures, and that he should never judge his reasonable creatures. (*The Works of Jonathan Edwards*, 2.884)

SOME REASONS HELL'S EXISTENCE IS REJECTED BY MANY

As surveys show, people are far more willing to believe in heaven than in hell. As a matter of fact, no good person wants anyone to go to hell. But as Sigmund Freud would say, it is an illusion to reject something simply because we *wish* not to believe in it. Indeed, as even some atheists have observed, belief in hell eliminates the charge that it is merely an illusion. Whether or not there is a hell must be determined on the basis of evidence, not desire. And again, the evidence for hell's existence is strong.

If the evidence for hell is substantial, why then do so many people reject it? Jonathan Edwards listed two main reasons: (1) It is contrary to our personal preference; (2) we have a deficient concept of evil and its deserved punishment.

Actually, denial of hell is an indication of human depravity. Edwards draws attention to our inconsistency. On the one hand we are all aware of the heinous nature of the torture of the Inquisition, Hitler's holocaust, Stalin's atrocities, and so on. On the other hand, while we are shocked by these horrors, why are we not equally shocked at how we regularly show contempt for God's majesty (*The Works of Jonathan Edwards*, 2.83)? In short, our rejection of hell and of God's mercy are an indication of our own depravity—and therefore we are deserving of hell.

Doth it seem to thee incredible, that God should be so utterly regardless of the sinner's welfare, as to sink him into an infinite abyss or misery? Is this shocking to thee? And is it not at all shocking to thee that thou shouldst be so utterly regardless as thou hast been to the honour and glory of the infinite God? (*The Works of Jonathan Edwards*, 2.82)

The Bible describes hell's reality in many forceful figures of speech. It is said to be "under the earth" (Philippians 2:10) and a place of outer darkness (Matthew 8:12; 22:13), which is "outside" [the gate of the heavenly city] (Revelation 22:14–15). Hell is away from the "presence of the Lord" (Matthew 25:41; 2 Thessalonians 1:7–9). Of course, "down" and "outside" are relational terms, not necessarily spatial ones. God is "up" and hell is "down." God is "inside" and hell is "outside." Hell is the other direction from God.

The nature of hell is a horrifying reality. It is like being left outside in the dark forever (Matthew 8:12; Jude 13). It is like a wandering star (Jude 13), clouds without rain (Jude 12), a perpetually burning dump (Mark 9:43–48), a bottomless pit (Revelation 20:1, 3), an everlasting prison (1 Peter 3:19), and a place of anguish and regret (Luke 16:28).

To borrow the title of a great book on hell, it is like a "great divorce"—an eternal separation from God (2 Thessalonians 1:7–9). There is, in biblical language, "a great gulf fixed" between hell and heaven (Luke 16:26 NKJV); no one can pass from one side to the other.

It is noteworthy that nowhere does the Bible describe it as a "torture chamber" where people are forced against their will to be tormented. This is a caricature created by unbelievers in order to justify their reaction to it by making God look cruel. A loving God (1 John 4:16) would not torture anyone.

This does not mean hell isn't a place of torment; Jesus said that it is (Luke 16:24). But unlike torture inflicted from without, against one's will, this torment is *self*-inflicted *by* one's will. As has been noted even by atheists (see Sartre, *No Exit and Three*

Other Plays), the door of hell is locked on the inside, its inhabitants condemned to their own freedom. Torment is living with the consequences of our own bad choices—it is the weeping and gnashing of teeth that results from the realization that we blew it and deserve the consequences. Just as a football player may pound on the ground and writhe in agony after a mistake that loses the Super Bowl, even so those in hell know that the pain they suffer is self-induced.

Hell is also depicted as a place of eternal fire. This fire is *real* but not necessarily *physical* (at least not as we know it), because people will have imperishable physical bodies (John 5:28–29; Revelation 20:13–15), so normal fire would not affect them. Further, the figures of speech that describe hell are contradictory, if taken in a physical sense. It has *flames,* yet is outer *darkness.* It is a *dump* or *chasm* (with a bottom), yet a *bottomless* pit. While everything in the Bible is literally true, not everything is true literally. For instance, God is not a literal rock (Psalm 18:2), since He is Spirit (John 4:24), but it is literally true that He is a solid, rocklike foundation we can trust.

THE ETERNAL DURATION OF HELL

Many unbelievers would be willing to accept a temporary hell, but the Bible speaks of it as everlasting. There are several lines of supporting evidence.

Hell Will Last as Long as God Does

The Bible declares that God will endure forever (Psalm 90:1–2), the beginning and the end (Revelation 1:8). He created all things (Colossians 1:15–16; John 1:3), and He will abide after this world is destroyed (2 Peter 3:10–12). But God by His very nature cannot tolerate evil (Isaiah 6; Habakkuk 1:13). Hence evil persons must be separated from God forever. As long as God is God and evil is evil, the latter must be separated from the former.

Hell Will Last as Long as Heaven Does

Heaven is described as "everlasting." The same Greek word (*aionion*), used in the same context, also affirms that hell is "eternal" or "everlasting" (Matthew 25:41; cf. 25:46; 2 Thessalonians 1:7–9; Revelation 20:10). If heaven is forever, then so is hell. There is absolutely no biblical ground for supposing that hell is temporal and heaven is eternal.

Likewise, there is no possibility of one getting out of hell once arriving there (Luke 16:26). Judgment begins immediately after death (Hebrews 9:27; John 8:21), and the result is everlasting, as cited above. This is not unlike some decisions in life being one-way and irreversible. Suicide, for instance, is a one-way street.

Furthermore, people are conscious after they die, whether they are in heaven (2 Corinthians 5:8; Philippians 1:23; Revelation 6:9) or in hell. The rich man is conscious in hell (Luke 16:24–26). The beast is still conscious after a thousand years in hell (Revelation 19:20; 20:10). Indeed, it makes no sense to resurrect unbelievers to everlasting judgment (Daniel 12:2; John 5:28–29) before the Great White Throne (Revelation 20:11ff.) in order to punish them for their sins unless they are conscious.

RESPONSE TO OBJECTIONS ABOUT HELL

Unbelievers have offered many objections to the doctrine of hell. Some of the more common ones will be briefly treated here.

The Objection That Hell Is Annihilation

It is objected that hell is not a place of eternal conscious punishment but one of eternal unconsciousness—annihilation. However, this is based on a misinterpretation of Scripture and is contrary to good reason.

First, the Bible clearly affirms there is conscious suffering in hell, such as "weeping and gnashing of teeth" (Matthew 8:12). By contrast, annihilated persons are not conscious of any suffering.

Second, the beast and false prophet in the lake of fire (where hell is thrown) are not annihilated, but still conscious after a thousand years of suffering, as cited above.

Third, annihilation would not be a punishment but a release from all punishment. Job preferred annihilation to suffering (Job 3), but God did not allow it. And if a good man like Job can suffer something worse than annihilation in this life, the punishment of evil people in the afterlife would have to be something greater. If not, then God is not just, since He would have given less punishment to the wicked than to the righteous.

Fourth, Jesus speaks of degrees of punishment in hell (Matthew 5:22). But there can be no degrees of annihilation. Nonexistence is the same for all persons. There are no degrees of nothingness.

Fifth, annihilation of the wicked is contrary to both the nature of God and the nature of humans made in His image (see "Immortality" in my *Baker Encyclopedia of Christian Apologetics*). It is not consistent with an all-loving God to snuff out those who do not do His wishes. What would we think of an earthly father who killed his children if they didn't do what he wanted them to do?

Finally, were God to annihilate human beings, He would be

attacking Himself. We are made in His image (Genesis 1:27), and God is immortal (1 Timothy 6:15−16). That these persons are suffering no more justifies annihilating them than it does for a parent to kill his child who is suffering. Even renowned atheists have insisted that annihilation is not to be preferred to conscious freedom. Nietzsche once wrote: "I would rather will nothingness than not to will at all" (*Toward a Genealogy of Morals*, last line).

The Objection That Hell Is Only Temporal, Not Eternal

In reply, hell could not be just a long imprisonment for several reasons. Hell must exist as long as a righteous God does, against whom all hell is opposed.

First, while the word *forever* can mean only "a long time" in some contexts, in this context it cannot, since it is used of heaven too (cf. Matthew 25:46). And heaven is not temporal; it is forever.

Second, sometimes the emphatic form of "forever and forever" is used. This same phrase is used to describe heaven and God Himself (Revelation 14:11; 20:10). And God cannot be temporal; He is eternal (*The Works of Jonathan Edwards,* 2.85–86).

Third, the suggestion that temporal suffering will lead to ultimate repentance is countered by several arguments. For one thing, the people in hell are gnashing their teeth, which does not indicate a godly and reformed disposition but a more rigid and stubborn rebellion. Hence after people have been in hell for some time, there is even more (not less) justification for God's punishment of them. Further, if hell has a reformatory effect on people, Jesus would not have pronounced woe on those who reject Him as being headed for hell (Matthew 11:21–24). Also, no sin would be unforgivable (cf. 12:31–32) if people in hell were reformable. Likewise, if people would repent in hell, Jesus would never have said of Judas that it would have been better if he'd never been born. Moreover, the extreme suffering in hell indicates God has no merciful intent toward the people there. A place of torment has no mercy in it. In addition, Jonathan Edwards asked how a place devoid of God's mercy can accomplish what no effort of His grace could accomplish on earth, namely, a change of the heart and disposition of wicked people. If hell could reform wicked sinners, then they would be saved without Christ, the sole means of salvation (*The Works of Jonathan Edwards*, 2.520). Suffering for those unwilling to reform has no tendency to soften a hard heart but actually hardens it more (cf. Pharaoh). The recidivism and hardened criminality in today's prisons confirm Edwards' point.

Finally, God's justice demands eternal punishment because "the heinousness of any crime must be gauged according to the worth or dignity of the person it is committed against" (see Davidson in *JETS*, 50). Thus, a murder of a president is more heinous than that of a terrorist or Mafia boss. Sin against an infinite God is infinite sin worthy of infinite punishment (*The Works of Jonathan Edwards*, 2.83).

Why Punish People—Why Not Reform Them?

Why eternal punishment? Why doesn't God try to reform sinners rather than punish them? The answer from both a biblical and rational point of view is simple. First, God does try to reform people; *the time of reformation is called life.* "The Lord is not slow in keeping his promise, as some understand slowness. He is patient with you, not wanting anyone to perish, but everyone to come to repentance" (2 Peter 3:9). However, *after the time of reformation comes the time of reckoning.* Again, "Man is destined to die once, and after that to face judgment" (Hebrews 9:27).

Further, hell is for the unreformable and unrepentant, the reprobate (cf. 2 Peter 2:1–2.). It is not for anyone who is reformable. If they *were*, they would still be alive. God in His wisdom and goodness would not allow anyone to go to hell whom He knew would go to heaven if He gave more opportunity (2 Peter 3:9); He "wants all men to be saved" (1 Timothy 2:4). C. S. Lewis observed, "The soul that seriously and constantly desires joy will never miss it. Those who seek find. To those who knock it is opened" (*The Great Divorce,* 69).

Moreover, God cannot force free creatures to be reformed. Forced reformation is worse than punishment; it is cruel and inhumane. At least punishment respects the person's freedom and dignity. "To be 'cured' against one's will . . . is to be put on a level with those who have not yet reached the age of reason or those who never will; to be classed with infants, imbeciles, and domestic animals" (Lewis, *God in the Dock,* 226). Humans are not objects to be manipulated; they are subjects to be respected because they are made in God's image. People should be punished when they do evil because they were free and knew better. They are *persons* to be punished, not *patients* to be cured.

Isn't Eternal Damnation for Temporal Sins Overkill?

To punish a person eternally for what he did on earth may seem like tremendous overkill. However, on closer examination it turns out to be not only just but necessary. For one thing, only eternal punishment will suffice for sins against an eternal God. Though the sins may have been committed in time, they were against the Eternal One. Furthermore, no sin can be tolerated as long as God exists, and He is everlasting. Hence punishment for sin must also be eternal.

Furthermore, God's only alternative to eternal punishment is worse, namely, to rob man of his freedom and dignity by either (1) forcing him into heaven against his free choice, which would be "hell" for him since he doesn't fit where everyone is loving and praising the Person he wants most to avoid, or (2) annihilating His own image within His creature, which would be an attack of God on himself.

As well, without an eternal separation there could be no heaven. Evil is contagious (1 Corinthians 5:6) and must be quarantined. Like a deadly plague, if not contained it will continue to contaminate and corrupt. If God did not eventually separate the tares from the wheat, the tares would choke out the wheat. The only way to preserve an eternal place of good is to eternally separate all evil from it. The only way to have an eternal heaven is to have an eternal hell.

Finally, if Christ's temporal punishment is sufficient for our sins eternally, there is no reason why eternal suffering cannot be appropriate for our temporal sins. It is not the *duration* of the action but the *object* that is important. Christ satisfied the eternal God by His temporal suffering (1 John 2:1–2), and unbelievers have defied the eternal God by their temporal sins.

The Objection That Hell Has No Redeeming Value

To this objection Jonathan Edwards answered that hell not only satisfies God's justice but glorifies it by showing how great and fearful a standard it is. "The vindicative justice of God will appear strict, exact, awful, and terrible, and therefore glorious" (*The Works of Jonathan Edwards*, 2.87). The more horrible and fearful the judgment, the brighter the sheen on the sword of God's justice. Awesome punishment fits the nature of an awesome God. By a majestic display of wrath, God recovers the majesty He has been refused. An awful display of punishment in the afterlife will bring to God what people refused to give Him in this life. Those who give God no glory by choice during this life will be forced to give Him glory in the afterlife.

Everyone is either actively or passively useful to God. In heaven believers will be actively useful in praising His mercy. In hell unbelievers will be passively useful in bringing majesty to God's justice. As Edwards put it, just as a barren tree is useful only for firewood, so disobedient people are only fuel for an eternal fire (*The Works of Jonathan Edwards*, 2.126). Since unbelievers prefer to keep at a distance from God in time, why should we not expect this to be their chosen state in eternity?

The Objection That Hell Is Only a Ruse

Some critics object that perhaps hell is only a threat God will not carry out. But it is blasphemy to hold that a God of truth would utilize a deliberate lie to govern human beings. Further, it implies that "those who think hell is a deception have outwitted God Himself by uncovering it" (see Davidson in *JETS*, 53). As Edwards stated it, "They suppose that they have been so cunning as to find out that it is not certain; and so that God had not laid his design so deep, but that such cunning men as they can discern the cheat and defeat the design" (*The Works of Jonathan Edwards*, 2.516).

How Can We Be Happy in Heaven Knowing a Loved One Is in Hell?

First, the very presupposition of this question is flawed. It supposes that we are more merciful than God! God is perfectly happy in heaven, and He knows that not everyone will be there, yet He is infinitely more merciful than we are. If we could not be happy in heaven knowing anyone was in hell, then our happiness is not in our hands but someone else's. But hell cannot veto heaven. We can be happy in heaven the same way we can be happy eating a delicious meal, knowing that others are starving. This is particularly so if we have tried to feed them but they have refused the food. And just as we can have healing of bad memories here on earth, even so God will wipe away all tears in heaven (Revelation 21:4).

Second, as Edwards noted, supposing God's mercy does not permit suffering in hell is contrary to fact. God allows plenty of suffering in this world. It is an empirical fact that God and creature-pain are not incompatible (Gerstner, *Jonathan Edwards on Heaven and Hell*, 80). If God's mercy could not bear eternal misery, then neither could it bear lesser amounts (*The Works of Jonathan Edwards*, 2.84).

Third, God's mercy is not a passion or emotion that negates His justice. Mercy so construed would be a defect in God. It would make Him weak and inconsistent with Himself, unfit to be a judge.

Fourth, our attitudes and feelings will be transformed and correspond to God's. Hence we will love only what God loves and hate what He hates. Since God is not miserable at the thought or sight of hell, neither will we be—even in the case of people we loved in this life. Edwards devoted a whole sermon to this: "The End of the Wicked Contemplated by the Righteous": "It will seem in no way cruel of God to inflict such extreme suffering on such extremely wicked creatures" (Gerstner, *Jonathan Edwards on Heaven and Hell*, 90).

Why Did God Create People He Knew Would Go to Hell?

Some critics argue that if God knew that His creatures would reject Him and eventuate in such a horrible place, why did He create them in the first place? Wouldn't it have been better to have never existed than to exist on earth and then go to hell?

In response, note that nonexistence cannot be said to be a better condition than any kind of existence, since nonexistence is nothing. Once again, to affirm that nothing can be better than something is a category mistake. In order to compare two things, they must have something in common, and there is nothing in common between being and nonbeing—they are diametrically opposed. Someone may *feel* like being put out of his misery, but it is contradictory to affirm that *nonbeing* is a better state of *being*.

Further, that some will lose in the game of life does not mean it should not be played. Before every driver in America takes to the road each day, we know that many people will be killed. Yet we will to allow people to drive, knowing tragic accidents will happen. Parents know that having children could end in great tragedy for their offspring as well as for themselves. Yet in all these cases our foreknowledge of evil does not negate our will to permit the possibility of good. We deem it worthwhile because it is better to have played with the opportunity to win than not to have played at all. From God's standpoint, it is better to have loved the whole world (John 3:16) and have lost some than not to have loved them at all.

Is It Just to Send People to Hell When They Can't Help Being Sinners?

The Bible says we are born sinners (Psalm 51:5) and are "by nature objects of wrath" (Ephesians 2:3). But sinners cannot avoid sinning, so is it fair to send them to hell for what they could not stop doing?

First of all, people go to hell for two reasons: (1) They are born with a bent to sin and (2) they choose to sin. They are born on a road that leads to hell, but they also fail to heed the warning signs along the way to turn from destruction (Luke 13:3; 2 Peter 3:9).

Furthermore, while humans sin because they are sinners (by nature), nonetheless, their sin nature does not force them to sin; they choose to sin. As Augustine correctly said, "We are born with the propensity to sin and the necessity to die." Notice he did not say we are born with the necessity to sin. While sin is *inevitable*, since we are born with a bent in that direction, nonetheless, sin is not *unavoidable*.

Likewise, the ultimate place to which sinners are destined is also avoidable. Indeed, each sin is avoidable by God's grace (1 Corinthians 10:13). *All sinners need to do is to repent* (Acts 17:30). All are held responsible for their decision to accept or reject God's offer of salvation, and responsibility always implies the ability to respond (if not on our own, then by God's grace).

All who go to hell could have avoided going there if they had chosen to do so. No pagan anywhere is without clear light from God so that he is "without excuse" (Romans 1:19–20; cf. 2: 12–15). Just as God sent a missionary to Cornelius (Acts 10:30–33), so He will provide the message of salvation for all who seek it. "Without faith it is impossible to please God, because anyone who comes to him must believe that he exists and that he rewards those who earnestly seek him" (Hebrews 11:6).

Chapter 10

What About Those Who Have Never Heard?

Orthodox Christianity faces yet another problem with regard to evil. Not only does it claim that not everyone will go to heaven (chapter 9), but it also claims that all those who do not accept Christ will go to hell. However, it seems that multimillions have never heard the gospel of Christ. That would mean God condemns people to eternal damnation who have never had a chance to be saved, and this seems to be incompatible with an all-loving God. Surely if God loved all, then He would make a way for all to be saved.

THE PROBLEM OF THE HEATHEN

The fate of those who have never heard is one of the most-asked questions by non-Christians. It is easily on the top-ten list, if not the top two or three.

The matter can be posed as follows:

1. God is all-loving.
2. An all-loving God wants all to be saved.
3. Christ is the only way to be saved.

4. But not everyone has heard about Christ.

5. Therefore, God cannot be all-loving.

If God were all-loving, He would get the message about Christ to all people. But much of the world is without the knowledge of how to be saved through Christ. Hence how can God be all-loving?

AN EVANGELICAL RESPONSE TO THE ARGUMENT FROM THE HEATHEN

There are two basic responses to this question by orthodox Christians: inclusivism and exclusivism. The first view (inclusivism) claims that while no one can be saved apart from the *work* of Christ, they can be saved without *knowing* about that work, providing they meet certain prerequisites. The second view (exclusivism) holds that they cannot be saved apart from the work of Christ, nor can they be saved without knowing about this work (called the gospel) and believing in it.

Inclusivism

Inclusivists sometimes speak of implicit faith—faith without explicitly knowing about Christ's work of salvation on our part, namely, His dying for our sins and rising again from the dead (1 Corinthians 15:1–4). Some believe this includes those who would have believed in Christ if they'd been given the opportunity to do so. So their faith is an implicit faith in Christ, even though they have never heard about Him.

This view is illustrated by someone receiving a gift of shoes addressed to them that are their size without knowing who the donor was or what price was paid for the shoes. Nor did they know what cow died to make the leather possible. Likewise, according to this view, Christ had to die and pay the price for our salvation (1 Peter 2:24; 3:18; Hebrews 10:14), but a person does not have to know this in order to be saved by Him. He simply needs to believe in God. As Hebrews 11:6 puts it, "Without faith it is impossible to please Him, for he who comes to God must believe that He is, and that He is a rewarder of those who diligently seek Him" (NKJV).

The Roman Catholic Vatican II Statement is a clear example of inclusivism:

> The plan of salvation also includes those who acknowledge the Creator, in the first place amongst whom are the Moslems. . . . Nor is God remote from those who in the shadow of images seek the unknown God. . . . Those who, through no fault of their own, do not know the Gospel of Christ or his Church, but who nevertheless seek God with sincere heart, and moved by grace, try in their actions to do his will as they know it through the dictates of their conscience—those too may achieve eternal salvation. (Vol. 1, 367)

Exclusivism

Like inclusivists, exclusivists too believe the work of Christ is absolutely essential to salvation. However, exclusivists, like myself, also hold that one must know about the work of Christ and believe it in order to be saved. We point to passages of Scripture like the following: "I am the way, the truth, and the life. No one comes to the Father except by me" (John 14:6); "Truly, truly, I say to you, he who does not enter the sheepfold by the door but climbs in another way is a thief and a robber. . . . I am the door. If anyone enters by me, he will be saved" (John 10:1, 9 ESV); "Unless you believe that I am he [the Messiah] you will die in your sins" (John 8:24 ESV); "Whoever believes in him is not condemned, but whoever does not believe is condemned already, because he has not believed in the name of the only Son of God" (3:18 ESV); "Salvation is found in no one else, for there is no other name under heaven given to men by which we must be saved" (Acts 4:12); "There is one God and one mediator between God and men, the man Christ Jesus" (1 Timothy 2:5).

For exclusivists, the problem of those who have never heard has an even greater intensity. How can God be all-loving if He condemns people to eternal hell who have not even had a chance to hear the plan of salvation?

1. Everyone Has General Revelation in Nature.

The reality is there is no one without revelation from God. The light of nature shines through to all

> since what may be known about God is plain to them, because God has made it plain to them. For since the creation of the world God's invisible qualities—his eternal power and divine nature—have been clearly seen, being understood from what has been made, so that men are *without excuse*. (Romans 1:19–20)

Further, everyone has general revelation in his heart.

> *All who have sinned without the law will also perish without the law,* and all who have sinned under the law will be judged by the law.... For when Gentiles, who do not have the law, by nature do what the law requires, they are a law to themselves, even though they do not have the law. They show that *the work of the law is written on their hearts.* (Romans 2:12–15 ESV)

These verses are reinforced by others that affirm that even the heathen have divine light (Acts 14), for "the heavens declare the glory of God; and the firmament shows His handiwork" (Psalm 19:1 NKJV). Thus Paul could speak to the Greeks about the so-called "Unknown God" whom they really know through His creation (Acts 17). All people have the light of creation and conscience.

This has been borne out by the classic twelve-volume work of the anthropologist Wilheim Schmidt, who demonstrated that originally, behind pagan (pre-literate) religions, was mono-theism (in his classic work, *The Origin of the Idea of God*, a definitive refutation of the widely dispersed evolutionary view of Frazer's *Golden Bough*). John Mbiti also has demonstrated original monotheism in his *African Religions and God*.

All of this confirms what Paul says in Romans:

> *Since the creation of the world God's invisible attributes—his eternal power and divine nature—have been clearly seen,* being understood from what has been made, so that men are without excuse. For *although they knew God,* they neither glorified him as God nor gave thanks to him, but their thinking became futile and their foolish hearts were darkened. Although they claimed to be wise, they became fools, and exchanged the glory of the immortal God for images made to look like mortal man and birds and animals and reptiles. (1:19–23)

2. No One Can Be Saved Apart From the Knowledge of Christ.

Salvation is not only through the work of Christ, but it comes to us only through knowledge about Christ. John declared that we must "enter" through the "door," who is Christ (John 10:1, 9; cf. 3:18; 8:24; Acts 4:12). It is not sufficient that Christ died for our sins; we must also "believe in the Lord Jesus" (Acts 16:31) to be saved. "How then shall they call on him in whom they have not believed? and how shall they believe in him of whom they have not heard? and how shall they hear without a preacher?" (Romans 10:14 KJV).

3. Everyone Who Seeks God Finds God.

As for those who have never heard, the Bible declares that if they seek God, God will get the message to them. Paul declares in Acts 17:26–28:

> He [God] made from one man every nation of mankind to live on all the face of the earth . . . *that they should seek God,* in the hope that they might feel their way toward him and find him. Yet he is actually not far from each one of us, for "In him we live and move and have our being" (ESV).

The writer of Hebrews added that "whoever would draw near to God must believe that he exists and that *he rewards those who seek him*" (11:6 ESV). Jeremiah said, *"You will seek me and find me, when you seek me with all your heart"* (Jeremiah 29:13 ESV). In fact, Peter announced that "in every nation *whoever fears Him and works righteousness is accepted by Him"* (Acts 10:35 NKJV), referring to Cornelius and his group.

> God, who made the world and everything in it, since He is Lord of heaven and earth, does not dwell in temples made with hands. Nor is He worshiped with men's hands, as though He needed anything, since He gives to all life, breath, and all things. And He has made from one blood every nation of men to dwell on all the face of the earth, and has determined their preappointed times and the boundaries of their dwellings, so that they should seek the Lord, in the hope that they might grope for Him and find Him, though *He is not far from each one of us;* for in Him we live and move and have our being, as also some of your own poets have said, "For we also are His offspring" (Acts 17:24–28 NKJV).

4. God Has Many Ways to Get the Message to Those Who Seek Him.

God knows in advance who will accept the message of the gospel, and He is not limited in how He can bring the gospel to them. The normative way should be through preaching (Matthew 28:18–20; Romans 10:14–17), but one can be saved through reading the Bible (Psalm 119:130; Hebrews 4:12). If necessary, God can get the message to one through angels (Revelation 14:6), or through visions (Daniel 4:5, 35), or through dreams (Daniel 2, 7). God also can speak from heaven through an audible voice (Acts 9) or through an inner voice in the heart as He did to the prophets (e.g., Hosea 1:1).

Some believe that the preaching of the message is the only way God does it because Jesus prayed, "I do not ask on behalf of these alone [the disciples], but for those also who believe in Me through their word" (John 17:20 NASB). However, in view of the above verses, it seems clear that God can use other ways if necessary. Even an angel will preach "the eternal gospel" (Revelation 14:6). If God could use dreams, visions, and angels to send His message on temporal matters, surely we cannot say that He would not do so for eternal matters if necessary.

I was in Eastern Europe before its doors were opened to the gospel. I heard of a Russian girl who was seeking God when a Bible fell out of a building at her feet; she picked it up, read it, and was saved! A number of years ago, I met a Chinese student who said he was seeking God but had no Bible in Chinese. Having heard of an English Bible in the library, he studied English for years, read the Bible, and came to believe in Christ. Some years ago, a native African was saved from his enemies, then was guided by a light out of the jungle to a missionary, who subsequently led him to Christ. Samuel Morris eventually came to

America and won many to the Lord. A book was written about him entitled *The March of Faith*. Many other similar stories have been told by missionaries and others (e.g., see A. H. Strong, *Systematic Theology*, 843–44).

There is no one anywhere who does not have revelation from God in nature (Romans 1:19–20) and in conscience (2:12–15). Rejecting this revelation is sufficient for condemnation but not for salvation. In order to be saved today[1] one must hear about Christ and believe in Him (Acts 4:12; 16:31). To those who have never heard about Christ yet are seeking Him, God will send a missionary, a tract, a Bible, or if necessary will give a dream, vision, or angelic message.

God is faithful, and those who seek Him find Him (Hebrews 11:6). But those who reject the light they have cannot expect God to give them more light. If someone is lost in the darkness of a jungle and sees even a small light, he should follow it. And if he does, it gets bigger. If he turns his back on the small light (of nature), he will find himself lost in the darkness. "Men loved darkness instead of light because their deeds were evil" (John 3:19). But all who seek the Light of the World may be enlightened to salvation by Him.

---

[1] For salvation in the Old Testament, see *Systematic Theology*, Vol. 4, chapter 17.

Animal Death
Before Adam

Paul said, "Through one man sin entered into the world, and death through sin, and so death spread to all men because all sinned [in Adam]" (Romans 5:12 NASB). God had warned Adam, "From any tree of the garden you may eat freely; but from the tree of the knowledge of good and evil you shall not eat, for in the day that you eat from it you will surely die" (Genesis 2:16–17 NASB). When he disobeyed, God said,

> Cursed is the ground because of you; in toil you will eat of it all the days of your life. Both thorns and thistles it shall grow for you; and you will eat the plants of the field; by the sweat of your face you will eat bread, till you return to the ground, because from it you were taken; for you are dust, and to dust you shall return. (3:17–19 NASB)

Paul adds,

> The creation was subjected to futility, not willingly, but because of Him who subjected it, in hope that the creation itself also will be set free from its slavery to corruption into the freedom of the glory of the children of God. For we know that the whole

creation groans and suffers the pains of childbirth together until now. (Romans 8:20–22 NASB)

However, according to the prevailing view in modern science, animals were dying many millions of years ago. According to the geological timetable, multi-cellular life appeared on earth about a half million years ago and has been dying ever since. If so, animals have been dying since long before Adam sinned. How then could their death be a result of Adam's sin?

SOME POSSIBLE SOLUTIONS TO THE PROBLEM OF ANIMAL DEATH

A common view among Christians is young-earth creationism. This became a widely held view in the wake of the publication of *The Genesis Flood* (1961) by Henry Morris and John Whitcomb. It was later disseminated through the Institute for Creation Research (ICR), founded by the late Henry Morris in 1970.

The Gap Theory

According to this view, there is a gap between the first two verses of the Bible where all the geological ages occurred. This position, popularized by the *Scofield Reference Bible*, posits a complete and perfect creation in the Bible's first verse, followed by the fall of Satan and the ruination of God's creation described in Genesis 1:2 as an earth that became "without form and void." This was succeeded by a re-creation of the world in Genesis 1:3ff. in six days.

In this way all the death in the animal kingdom before Adam was the result of the fall of Satan. Then later, in Genesis 3, Adam and Eve sinned and brought ruination on the Adamic race. Some Gap Theory proponents, such as G. H. Pember (in *Earth's Earliest Ages*), postulated a pre-Adamic race that fell between Genesis 1:1 and 1:2.

> We see, then, that God created the heavens and the earth perfect and beautiful in their beginning, and that at some subsequent period, how remote we cannot tell, the earth passed into a state of utter desolation and was void of all life. . . . But what could have occasioned so terrific a catastrophe? Wherefore had God thus destroyed the work of His hands? If we may draw any inference from the history of our own race, sin must have been the cause of this hideous ruin: sin, too, which would seem to have been patiently borne with through long ages until at length its cry increased to Heaven, and brought down utter destruction. (33)

This view is not widely held by Bible scholars today for several reasons. First, there is no grammatical indication of a gap between the first two verses of Genesis. It also is viewed as contrary to good Hebrew grammar to render Genesis 1:2 as "and the earth *became* without form and void." Second, there is no geological evidence in the fossil record for a gap between the animal fossils and Adam. Third, the verse used to show there was a pre-Adamic race is taken out of context; the reference in Jeremiah 4:23 (KJV) that uses the same phrase ("without form, and void") is not looking backward but forward to a future judgment of God. Fourth, it raises serious questions about redemption for this "pre-Adamic" race, since Christ died only for the Adamic race (1 Corinthians 15:45–49).

Young-Earth Flood Geology

Henry Morris's *Scientific Creationism* is a widely read defense of this position. More recently, Ken Ham has developed a following through his "Answers in Genesis" ministry and in the construction of a multimillion-dollar Creation Museum near Cincinnati. The essence of the young-earth view is as follows.

1. ALL DEATH (HUMAN AND ANIMAL) IS A DIRECT RESULT OF THE FALL.

The Bible says explicitly that "just as through one man sin entered into the world, and death through sin, and so *death spread to all men, because all sinned* [in Adam]" (Romans 5:12 NASB). *"The creation was subjected to futility. . . . The whole creation groans and suffers the pains of childbirth together until now"* (8:20–22 NASB).

2. THE FOSSIL RECORD IS A RESULT OF THE FLOOD.

According to this view, the fossil record of past animal death poses no problem, since this death all occurred after the fall—after the flood. This of course entails a young- earth (only thousands of years) as opposed to an old-earth view (billions of years), held by virtually the entire scientific community (including many Bible-believing Christians).

Critics present biblical arguments in favor of longer time periods than six solar days of creation (e.g., see Stoner, *A New Look at an Old Earth*). In addition, they use the evidence of science for long periods of time, including the speed of light and radioactive decay processes. These are rejected by young-earth proponents in favor of an earth no more than six to ten thousand years old.

3. THE "DAYS" OF GENESIS ARE TWENTY-FOUR-HOUR DAYS.

According to the young-earth view, the creation of the universe occurred in 144 hours, or six successive twenty-four-hour days. Accordingly, all death of animals occurred after the fall of Adam and resulted from it. In this view, no other explanation is needed to account for physical calamities, sickness, and death. Adam's sin precipitated it all.

Usually this view holds a closed chronology, where few or no gaps are allowed between persons in the basic geological tables (Genesis 5 and 10). By adding the numbers, one arrives at a date around 4000 BC, placing the creation about six thousand years ago.

Opponents point to gaps in the genealogies, such as the three generations (of 1 Chronicles 3:11–15) left out between Jehoram and Uzziah in Matthew 1:8. They also note that Jesus' genealogy in Luke 3:36 contains the name *Cainan*, not found in Genesis 11, thus leaving a gap in the Genesis genealogy. Some add that the term *day* in Genesis 2:3 refers to more than a twenty-four-hour day, and the "seventh day," on which God rested, is still going on over six thousand years later, according to Hebrews 4:3–6.

The Old-Earth Views

Those who reject the young-earth view believe animals were dying millions of years before Adam fell. If animal death *is* a result of Adam's sin, then how could animals have been dying before he sinned?

THE ANTICIPATORY VIEW

Until recently, it was common for old-earth viewers to argue that animal death was not the result of Adam's fall—that Romans 5:12 does not really say animals died as a result of Adam's sin. It says, literally, "sin entered the world through one man, and death through sin, and in this way death came to *all men.*" Further, Romans 8 does not say animals died because of Adam's sin, but simply that "the creation was subjected to frustration" and "to decay" and "groaning" since the fall (vv. 20–22).

Why then was there animal death before the human fall? Several possibilities have been offered. For one, it was simply part of God's overall order of creation, where higher animals live off of lower ones. It had no moral implications because there were no moral beings millions of years before there were human beings.

Some point to the fact that the garden of Eden was a limited space with a way in (Genesis 3:24) and presumed fence or enclosure, since it would make no sense to have an opening without a closed-in area. Hence when Adam and Eve were expelled, this more difficult world in which to live was already there, since God had anticipated their fall.

THE RETROACTIVE VIEW

More recently, William Dembski has proposed another fascinating alternative. He argues (in *The End of Christianity: Finding a Good God in an Evil World*) that just as God provided salvation before the cross from the "foundation of the world" (Revelation 13:8; Ephesians 1:4) based on the future work of Christ, even so, God pronounced condemnation and death on the animal kingdom before Adam sinned—which condemnation was a result of Adam's sin yet to come.

> God's response to the "big fire" of the Fall [yet to come] is like the anticipatory action of firefighters in setting backfires. . . . [Thus,] if we accept that God acts to anticipate the Fall, the world has already experienced the consequences of human sin in the form of natural evil. (170, 173)

This view has the advantage of taking both the Genesis 3 and Romans 8 passages as affirming that animal death, as well as human death, is a result of Adam's fall just as the young-earth view holds. Yet Dembski's view also accommodates the dominant perspective of modern science and old-earth creationists who maintain animal death millions of years before Adam. Of course, like the other models, it is an attempt to give a Bible-based answer to the age-old problem of natural evil before Adam.

There are a number of ways to account for the death of animals before the fall. The pre-Adamic race seems the least probable, and the retroactive view is the most creative. As to which is most probable, the determining factor will be the age of the earth. Without attempting to resolve that longstanding difference of view, we at least can conclude that all of the views, if true, would account for the presence of animal death, whether it occurred before or after the fall of humankind.

Evidence for the Existence of God

Christianity, a theistic religion, holds that there is one personal, moral, infinite Being beyond the universe who created it. Atheists argue that the problem of evil is evidence God does not exist. But evil actually presupposes the existence of God, for there is no way to know there is injustice in the world unless one has an objective standard of justice beyond the world by which he knows the world is not just. An ultimate moral law implies an Ultimate Moral Lawgiver (God). So atheism's "best" argument against God turns out to be an argument for God.

In addition, there are many good arguments for the existence of a theistic God.

The following is a summary of the main ones. Given these good reasons that God exists, there likewise is more evidence of a solution to the problem of evil. If an infinitely powerful, infinitely knowing, and infinitely perfect Being exists, then there is overarching evidence that He has both the will and the ability to control and conquer evil.

THE COSMOLOGICAL ARGUMENTS FOR GOD'S EXISTENCE

The word *cosmological* comes from *kosmos* (universe) and *logos* (reason for). There are two forms of the cosmological argument: one deals with the beginning of the universe (the horizontal argument), and the other deals with the existence of the universe right now (the vertical argument).

Forms of the Horizontal (Kalam)[1] Argument for God

The outline of the horizontal argument is very simple:

1. Whatever had a beginning, had a Beginner (Cause).
2. The universe had a beginning.
3. Therefore, the universe had a Beginner (Cause).

The first premise is based on the principle of causality: "Everything that comes to be had a cause." Nothing comes from nothing; nothing ever could. Famous physicist Stephen Hawking claims in his recent book *The Grand Design* (Bantam, 2010) that the universe came into existence spontaneously without a cause. But this is the ultimate absurdity in which there is a creation and no Creator, a grand design with no Grand Designer, and by which nothing produced something—the whole universe! Even the skeptic David Hume said, "I never asserted so absurd a proposition as that any thing might arise without a cause: I only maintained that our certainty of the falsehood of that proposition

---

[1] *Kalam* is the Arabic word for "eternal." Several medieval Arabian philosophers (like al-Ghazali and al-Kindi) defended this argument, as did the medieval Christian philosopher Bonaventure. A strong contemporary evangelical defense is found in William Lane Craig's *The Kalam Cosmological Argument*.

proceeded neither from intuition nor demonstration, but from another source."[2]

The second premise is supported by both scientific and rational evidence.

Scientifically, the second law of thermodynamics states that in a closed isolated system (such as the whole universe is) the amount of useable energy is decreasing. In short, the universe is running out of useable energy. As agnostic astrophysicist Robert Jastrow said,

> Once hydrogen has been burned with that star and converted to heavier elements, it can never be restored to its original state. Minute by minute and year by year, as hydrogen is used up in stars, the supply of this element in the universe grows smaller.[3]

Furthermore, like with an hourglass, where the sand is pouring from the top to the bottom, we know that if all the sand is not in the bottom, the hourglass has not been there forever. Likewise, since the universe has not yet run out of useable energy, it follows that the universe is not eternal—it had a beginning. Everything that had a beginning had a cause. Therefore, the universe had a cause (God).[4]

Since the Cause of the universe is beyond the finite universe, it must not be finite (i.e., infinite). And since it is beyond the whole natural universe, it must be supernatural. As Jastrow put it, "That there are what I or anyone would call supernatural

---

[2]David Hume, *Letters* I, 187.

[3]Robert Jastrow, *God and the Astronomers*, 15–16.

[4]Many scientists offer other evidence that the universe had a beginning: e.g., the expanding universe, microwave radiation, Einstein's general theory of relativity, and the great mass of energy discovered by the Hubble telescope. This "Big Bang" evidence has convinced most astrophysicists that the physical universe must have had a beginning. Even if some of this evidence is disputed, the whole argument rests on the indisputable evidence of the second law, for which there are no known exceptions.

forces at work is now, I think, a scientifically proven fact."[5] He adds elsewhere,

> The scientist's pursuit of the past ends in the moment of creation. This is an exceedingly strange development, unexpected by all but theologians. They have always accepted the word of the Bible: "In the beginning God created the heavens and the earth."[6]

There is also a philosophical argument for the beginning of the universe:

1. Everything that began had a cause.
2. The temporal universe had a beginning.
3. Therefore, the temporal universe had a Cause (God).

Time, as a series of one moment after another, cannot be eternal. Why? Because, by definition, *an infinite series never ends.* But the present moment is the end of all the moments before it. Therefore, there could not have been an infinite number of moments before today. Time must have had a beginning. And if the temporal world had a beginning, then it must have had a Cause (God).

So both the scientific evidence and sound reason lead to an infinite supernatural Cause of the space-time universe's origin. This is what theism means by "God."

The Vertical Form of the Cosmological Argument for God

This argument answers the age-old question: Why is there something rather than nothing—right now? In other words,

---

[5] Jastrow, in an interview in *Christianity Today,* 15.
[6] Jastrow, *God and the Astronomers,* 115.

what is causing the universe to exist currently? The argument can be stated in different ways. The classical way is this:[7]

1. Every contingent (dependent) being has a cause right now.
2. The whole physical universe is contingent right now.
3. Therefore, the whole physical universe has a Cause right now.

The first premise is another form of the principle of causality, for whatever is contingent (dependent) does not account for its own existence. Why? Because it is dependent in its being, and whatever is dependent in its being is dependent on something else for its being. To put it another way, whatever is contingent in its being could possibly not exist; that is, it has the potentiality for nonexistence. So whatever does exist, but could possibly not exist, does not explain why it exists rather than not exist.

The whole universe could possibly not exist: Its nonexistence is possible.[8] Hence the whole universe needs a cause for its existence—right now. But the cause of a contingent being cannot itself be a contingent being, or else it too would need a cause. Hence the Cause of the whole contingent world must be a non-contingent being, that is, a necessary Being (God).

Another way to put this argument is in terms of the parts and the whole.

1. Every part of the universe needs a cause.
2. The whole is the sum of all the parts.
3. Therefore, the whole universe needs a Cause (God).

---

[7]See Thomas Aquinas, *Summa Theologica*, 1.2.3 ("Third Way").

[8]That is, there is nothing contradictory about the nonexistence of everything. A total state of nothingness is a possible state of affairs.

No part of the universe is self-sustaining. Each part is dependent on something else for its existence. There are no uncaused parts, no matter what "part" is taken to mean (molecules, atoms, physical energy, whatever). In more scientific terms, there is no part composed of unlimited energy, energy that is not running down. According to the second law (above), all matter in the universe is running out of useable energy. So every part of the universe is dependent or caused. Because the whole is equal to the sum of all the parts, if every part is caused, then the whole universe is caused as well.

Opponents sometimes object to this as the fallacy of composition, which argues that the whole does not always have the same characteristics as the parts. For example, a square can be made of two triangles. But each part is a triangle, and the whole is a square.

In response, theists point out that if both parts are geometric figures, then by its very nature the whole is a geometric figure. And if each tile on the floor is brown, then the whole floor is brown. It is not essential, but accidental, to triangles that adding them together does not always make a triangle. But it is essential to the very nature of a contingent part that adding up all of them does not equal a necessary Being. No matter how many contingent parts are in the whole, the whole sum of them is still contingent.

One way to understand this is to ask a simple question: If all the parts of the universe are taken away, would there be anything left? If not, then the whole universe is equal to the sum of all its parts and, therefore, it is caused. If something *is* left when all the parts are gone, then it must be something more than the contingent, temporal, or caused universe: It must be a transcendent, necessary, eternal, and uncaused Being on which every part of the universe is dependent for its existence! So either way (whether or not the parts are equal to the whole), every part in the universe needs a cause (God), and so does the whole universe.

Some theists have offered another brief argument for God. It goes like this:

1. Something exists (e.g., I do).
2. But nothing cannot cause something.
3. Therefore, an eternal and necessary Being exists (God).

It must be eternal, since if ever there were nothing, then there would always be nothing, since nothing cannot cause something. It must be necessary, for all beings cannot be contingent (dependent); there must be a necessary Being on which they depend for their existence. Thus since I undeniably exist, it follows that there must be an eternal necessary Being that is the ground for my existence (and anything else that may exist).[9]

THE TELEOLOGICAL ARGUMENTS FOR GOD'S EXISTENCE

The Greek word *telos* means "end, purpose, or design." Reasoning from design is called the teleological argument for God. It has many forms, but the most recent scientific evidence for it comes from two main sources.

The Anthropic Principle

One of the most important recent scientific discoveries is the anthropic principle (from the Greek *anthropos*, "human

---

[9]Some have claimed that this argument does not disprove pantheism. In short, it only proves that I exist and that an eternal necessary Being exists—maybe I am God. However, this "hole" can be plugged quickly by pointing out that (1) I change, (2) God does not change, and (3) hence I am not God. The pantheist acknowledges that he changes because he did not always think he was God. But God did. Accordingly, the pantheist is not God.

being"). According to this principle, from the very inception of the universe it was fine-tuned or tweaked for the eventual emergence of human life.[10] There are over one hundred factors that must be in perfect balance in order for human life to exist. These include: (1) 21 percent oxygen in the air is just right for life (more and we would burn up, less and we would suffocate); (2) the sun is just the right distance from the earth (closer and we would burn up, farther and we would freeze); (3) the tilt of the earth is just right for life (otherwise it would get too cold at night and too hot in the day); (4) the gravitational force is just right to make movement possible but to keep us from flying off into space; (5) the position of Jupiter is just right to protect the earth from cosmic bodies destroying us; (6) the nuclear force is just right to hold the atoms together, and so on—dozens and dozens of factors make human life possible.[11]

This evidence has been put together beautifully in a book (and DVD) entitled *The Privileged Planet* by Guillermo Gonzalez. Robert Jastrow summed up the situation well:

> The anthropic principle is the most interesting next to the proof of the creation, and it is even more interesting because it seems to say that science itself has proven, as a hard fact, that this universe was made, was designed, for man to live in. It is a very theistic result.[12]

Why is it a theistic result? Because it points to a theistic God beyond the whole universe who planned the emergence of human life and who tweaked the universe just right from the very beginning to make it possible.

---

[10]See J. D. Barrow, *The Anthropic Cosmological Principle,* for the most detailed description.
[11]See Hugh Ross, *The Creator and the Cosmos,* 111–121.
[12]Robert Jastow, interview in *Christianity Today,* 17.

1. Advanced planning is a sign of an intelligent cause.
2. The whole universe shows evidence of advanced planning.
3. Hence the whole universe was planned by an Intelligent Cause (God).[13]

When contemplating the nature of the universe's physical laws alone, Albert Einstein said, "The harmony of natural law . . . reveals an intelligence of such superiority that, compared with it, all the systematic thinking and acting of human beings is an utterly insignificant reflection."[14] Likewise, former atheist Allan Sandage, who did the expanding-universe study on the Mount Palomar telescope, said,

> The world is too complicated in all of its parts to be due to chance alone. I am convinced that the existence of life with all its order in each of its organisms is simply too well put together. . . . The more one learns of biochemistry the more unbelievable it becomes unless there is some kind of organizing principle—an architect for believers.[15]

Scientist Michael Behe encapsulated the evidence: What we have is a planet in the right regions of a solar system, in the right region of a galaxy, in a universe with the right kind of laws to produce chemicals with the right kind of properties—This is all necessary for life, but still very far from sufficient. The planet itself has to be not too big and not too small, with enough but not too much water, the right kind of minerals in the right place. . . .

---

[13] Atheists sometimes respond to the anthropic principle by saying that the universe being here is proof that it just happened that way, otherwise it would not be here. But this is like arguing that a painting does not need a painter because it would not look like a painting if all the colors and pigments were not the way they just happen to be.

[14] Cited by Fred Heeren, *Show Me God*, 66.

[15] Allan Sandage, cited in *Truth*, 54.

All are critical. If any one of them were missing, intelligent life would be precluded.[16]

The critical prearrangement of so many parts, all co-conspiring for the same end, is always a sign of intelligent design. We never observe natural laws doing such a thing.

The Argument From Microbiology

In Darwin's day a living cell was considered a "black box," since they did not have microscopes capable of seeing into the cell's secrets. In *Darwin's Black Box*, Michael Behe started a design revolution. After narrating the evidence for the incredible complexity of a living cell, the microbiologist concluded:

> The conclusion of intelligent design flows naturally from the data itself—not from sacred books or sectarian beliefs. Inferring that biochemical systems were designed by an intelligent agent is a humdrum process that requires no new principles of logic or science. [So] life on earth at its most fundamental level, in its most critical components, is the product of intelligent activity.[17]

In a more recent book, Behe updates his argument, showing that life is even more complex than first thought.[18]

The atheist Nobel laureate Francis Crick admitted,

> An honest man, armed with all the knowledge available to us now, could only state that in some sense, the origin of life appears at the moment to be almost a miracle, so many are the conditions which would have to have been satisfied to get it going.[19]

---

[16]Michael Behe, *The Edge of Evolution*, 212.
[17]Michael Behe, *Darwin's Black Box*, 193.
[18]Behe, *The Edge of Evolution*.
[19]Francis Crick, *Life Itself: Its Origin and Nature*, 88.

Former atheist Sir Fred Hoyle stated the matter this way:

> Biochemical systems are exceedingly complex, so much so that the chance of their being formed through random shuffling of simple organic molecules is exceedingly minute, to a point indeed where it is insensibly different from zero. [So there must be] an intelligence, which designed the biochemicals and gave rise to the origin of carbonaceous life.[20]

Even the renowned atheist Richard Dawkins has admitted that life appears to have been designed and that an original one-celled animal has a thousand sets of encyclopedias full of genetic information in it![21] But where could all this complex information have come from, except from an intelligent Designer of first life?

THE BIOLOGICAL ARGUMENT FROM SPECIFIED COMPLEXITY

Life is unique; it has what scientists call "specified complexity." Crystals are specified but not complex, having only a simple message repeated over and over. Random polymers are complex but not specified, carrying no real message at all. Only life is *both* specified and complex. Claude Shannon developed an information theory for Bell Labs, showing that the information carrying letters have a certain letter frequency. Herbert Yockey applied this to the DNA in living cells and discovered there is a mathematical identity between the letter sequence in DNA and that of a human language: "The sequence hypothesis applies directly to the protein and the genetic text as well as to

---

[20] Sir Fred Hoyle, *Evolution from Space*, 3, 143.
[21] Richard Dawkins, *The Blind Watchmaker,* 17–18, 116.

written languages and therefore the treatment is mathematically identical."[22]

This leads to the following argument:

1. Wherever we observe specified complexity in the present (such as in human language), it is caused by an intelligent cause.[23]
2. The specified complexity in a living cell is mathematically identical to that in a human language.
3. Therefore, first life must have had an intelligent cause.

Notice that it is *not the absence of a natural cause* that leads to this conclusion—it is *the presence of evidence for an intelligent cause* that does. So positing an intelligent cause of first life is not the God-of-the-gap fallacy, as many atheists charge. For example, it is not the lack of known natural causes that leads us to posit an intelligent cause of the faces on Mount Rushmore, or a sand castle on the beach. Rather, it is known evidence for an intelligent cause from previous experience that leads to the conclusion of an intelligent cause for these specified forms. The same is true of the specified form of first life.

For instance, Carl Sagan and the SETI (Search for Extra-Terrestrial Intelligence) program depict (in the movie *Contact*) scientists who were elated when they received one message (all prime numbers 1 to 100) on the radio telescope. As Sagan put it, "The receipt of a single message from outer space would show that it is possible to live through such technological

---

[22] Herbert Yockey, *The Journal of Theoretical Biology,* 91.

[23] If the atheist rejects this premise, then he has rejected the very principle of uniformity by which we know the past, namely, that the kind of causes we see repeatedly producing a certain kind of effect in the present is the same kind of cause we should posit for producing it in the past. Without this principle there is no science of the past. So the theist's reasoning to an intelligent cause of first life is scientific, but the opposing view is not.

adolescence"[24] because it would have proved there was an intelligent civilization out there. Ironically, the same man said elsewhere that the human brain is so complex that it has twenty million volumes full of genetic information in it. Sagan wrote, "The neuro-chemistry of the brain is astonishingly busy, the circuitry of a machine more wonderful than any devised by humans."[25] If so, and if it takes an intelligent being to form one simple message, how much greater Mind did it take to create a human brain with the equivalent of the Library of Congress in it!

After reviewing the scientific evidence for God, the most notorious former atheist of modern times, Antony Flew, concluded:

> Those scientists who point to the Mind of God do not merely advance a series of arguments or a process of syllogistic reasoning. Rather, they propound a vision of reality that emerges from the conceptual heart of modern science and imposes itself on the rational mind. It is a vision that I personally find compelling and irrefutable.[26]

THE MORAL ARGUMENT FOR GOD'S EXISTENCE

In addition to the cosmological arguments, which point to an infinite supernatural Cause of the universe, and the teleological argument, which shows that this Cause is also a super-intelligent Being, the moral argument reveals a God who is morally perfect. It takes the following form:

1. Every moral law has a moral lawgiver.
2. There is an objective moral law.

---

[24] Carl Sagan, *Broca's Brain*, 275.

[25] Carl Sagan, *Cosmos*, 278.

[26] Antony Flew, *There Is a God: How the World's Most Notorious Atheist Changed His Mind*, 112.

3. Therefore, there must be an objective Moral Lawgiver.

The first premise is self-evident. Laws have lawgivers, and prescriptions have prescribers. The burden of proof rests on the second premise. What is the evidence that there is an objective moral law, not just something subjective or created by humans? Strangely enough, atheists themselves have provided the evidence for a moral law—evidence so strong that it has converted many of them to belief in a Lawgiver (God).

The most famous form of this argument was stated by C. S. Lewis.[27] As a former atheist, Lewis believed that the evil and injustices in the world eliminated God. But then he asked himself:

> Just how had I got this idea of just and unjust? A man does not call a line crooked unless he has some idea of a straight line. What was I comparing this universe with when I called it unjust? . . . Of course I could have given up my idea of justice by saying it was nothing but a private idea of my own. But if I did that, then my argument against God collapsed too—for the argument depended on saying that the world was really unjust, not simply that it did not happen to please my private fancies. Thus in the very act of trying to prove that God did not exist—in other words, that the whole of reality was senseless—I found I was forced to assume that one part of reality—namely my idea of justice—was full of sense.[28]

Lewis is not the only atheist to come this route. Former Nietzschean atheist J. Budziszewski came to God the same way. He reasoned,

> What actually led me back was a growing intuition that my condition was objectively evil. . . . Evil is deficiency in good; there is

[27] See C. S. Lewis, *Mere Christianity,* part 1.
[28] Lewis, *Mere Christianity,* 45–46.

no such thing as an evil "substance," an evil-in-itself. So if my condition really was evil, there had to be some good of which my condition was the ruination. In short, we cannot know evil except on the backdrop of good. If evil is real, then there must be an objective standard by which we know that.[29]

Former atheist (now head of the human genome project) Francis Collins was impressed with the moral argument on his way back to God. He later wrote,

> After twenty-eight years as a believer, the Moral Law still stands out for me as the strongest signpost to God. More than that, it points to a God who cares about human beings, and a God who is infinitely good and holy.[30]

There are many reasons that there must be an objective moral law:

1. We would not know there was injustice unless there were an objective standard of justice.

2. True progress is not possible unless we know an objective standard by which we measure that things are getting better or worse. We can't know better unless we know what is best.

3. Real moral disagreements are not possible without an objective moral standard. But there *are* real moral disagreements—for example, those about injustice, intolerance, and cruelty.

4. The same basic moral codes are found in most cultures.[31]

---

[29] J. Budziszewski, "Objections, Obstacles, Acceptance."
[30] Francis Collins, *The Language of God,* 218.
[31] See C. S. Lewis, *The Abolition of Man,* appendix.

5. Guilt from breaking a moral law would not be universal if there were no objective moral law.

6. Even those who deny moral absolutes have moral principles they believe are universal, such as tolerance, freedom of expression, and the wrongness of bigotry and genocide.

7. We did not invent the moral law any more than we invented mathematical or physical laws. It is discovered, not created.

8. We sometimes choose duty (e.g., to save a drowning person) over instinct (not to risk our own life).

9. The basic moral law is discovered not by how we behave, but by how we desire others to behave toward us.

10. Acts of altruism cannot be adequately explained naturalistically.

I know of a student who claimed he was a moral relativist in a well-researched, well-documented term paper until the professor marked it with these words: "F. I don't like blue folders!" The student sharply complained that it was unjust, unfair, and flat-out not right to give him an F simply because of the color of the folder. And the student was right. But he was right in his protest only because he was wrong in his paper. There is an objective moral principle that says it is wrong to fail a student because of the color of the folder and not based on the content of the paper.

Lewis points out that the "moral law" cannot be herd instinct, or else we would always act from the strongest impulse, but we don't. Our moral duty sometimes trumps even mother love and patriotism. Neither can the moral law be mere social convention, because the moral law sometimes condemns well-established conventions like Nazism. Nor can the moral law be identified as the laws of nature, since they are merely descriptive, not prescriptive.

Sometimes things factually more convenient are deemed morally worse. For example, a person who tries to crash into my car but fails is held to be worse than someone who accidentally does run into my car. Also, the moral law can't be mere fancy, because we can't get rid of it even when we want to do so, any more than we can get rid of the mathematical tables when we make a mistake in multiplying. The moral law can no more be part of nature than an architect can be part of the building he designs. It is prescriptive, not descriptive, and every moral prescription needs a Moral Prescriber.[32]

RESPONDING TO SOME OBJECTIONS

This is not to say atheists do not give objections to belief in God, only that they offer no rationally valid ones. In truth, many are worn out and retreaded. Even intellects the size of Richard Dawkins employ amateuristic protests that were answered centuries ago.

Objection One: If everything needs a cause, then so does God. If God does not need a cause, then neither does the universe.

Response: This is a misstatement of the principle of causality. The theist does not argue that every *thing* [being] needs a cause; rather, all *effects* need causes. Only finite, contingent things having a beginning need a cause, since they do not explain why they exist when they need not exist. Hence the universe of finite, contingent things needs a cause. But God does not have a beginning, nor is He finite, so He does not need a cause.

Only effects need causes. No Cause as such needs a cause.

---

[32]See Lewis, *Mere Christianity*, part 1.

In fact, to posit that every cause needs a cause is to claim that the "cause" needing a cause is really an effect. But this begs the whole question by assuming what is to be proven by making it impossible to ever get to a Cause of what is being caused. Sculptures need sculptors, but sculptors do not need sculptors. They are the sculptors.

Objection Two: An endless series of causes is possible. Hence there is no First Cause (God).

Response: An endless series of causes before today is not possible for two reasons.

First, there cannot be an endless series of any finite things because an infinite (endless) series has no end. Today is the end of all days leading up to today. Hence there cannot be an infinite number of causes before today. Of course, there can be an infinite number of *abstract points* between A and B. But abstract points are not *concrete things*. Thus there is an infinite number of abstract points between the two ends of a bookshelf. But one cannot get an infinite number of actual books in there, no matter how thin they are. Likewise, an infinite number of real causes is impossible.

Second, in every series of essential causes, every cause is being caused. Otherwise, there would be an uncaused Cause (God), which the series is trying to avoid. Further, in every such series of causes of being, at least one cause is causing—otherwise there would be no causality in the series. But in this case, this one cause would be causing itself (since it is both causing and being caused), which is impossible. A cause is prior in being to its effect, but no cause can be prior in being to itself, actually or logically.

Finally, as Lewis wisely observed, an infinite regress is a futile attempt to explain away the need for explanation itself. It is saying in effect that nothing is really a cause; everything is only an effect. But everything can't be an effect, since an effect is by definition the result of a cause.

Objection Three: Assuming God is like intelligent causes in the present does not lead to a theistic God but to a humanlike cause or causes, the same kind of causes we see producing these kinds of things in the present. A car does not need a carmaker, since we know there are many workers that produce cars. So at best the design argument would prove polytheism (many finite gods), not monotheism (one infinite God).

Response: The principle of uniformity (based on knowing the kind of cause that produces something in the present) does not demand an *identical* cause in the past but a *similar* one to what we observe in the present. The SETI program did not demand that extraterrestrials were the *same* as humans but only that their intelligence was *similar* to ours. Further, the cause does not have to be similar in any bodily way but only in that it has human*like* intelligence. Experience in the present informs us that an airplane does not need a designer who is in material and shape like an airplane. Further, a Creator cannot be the same as a creature. The Creator is infinite (unlimited) and the creature is finite (limited). Hence attributing a body or bodily parts (all of which are limited) to the Creator is as unjustified as attributing matter in a vase to a mind that formed it.

Objection Four: The arguments given for God do not prove that there is only one God, as theists claim there is.

Response: There can only be one God according to these arguments.

First, the God of the cosmological argument is infinite,[33]

---

[33] God has to be infinite since every finite being needs a cause. Hence the Cause of all finite beings must not be finite (i.e., infinite). If He were finite, then He would need a cause and not be the Cause of every finite being (which does need a cause).

since *every* finite thing needs a cause. Hence the Cause of finite things must not be finite (i.e., infinite). And there cannot be two infinite Beings, for in order for there to be two beings of the same kind, they would have to differ. Two infinite Beings do not differ; they are the same kind of Being, namely, infinite.

Second, the theistic God (of the moral argument) is absolutely perfect, and there cannot be two absolutely perfect beings. To be different, one would have to have a perfection the other did not have, and the one that lacked that perfection would not be absolutely perfect. Hence there can be only one absolutely perfect Being.

Third, the teleological argument (according to the anthropic principle) shows there was one Mind behind the whole universe doing all the preplanning.

Finally, there is only one set of physical laws in the whole universe, which reflects one Mind behind it all. It is a uni-verse (one world from one Mind), not a multi-verse (many worlds from many minds).

FINAL THOUGHTS

The various arguments for God show there is only one God, not many. This God must be infinite, since He is beyond the finite world He made. Further, He must be personal, because He is both intelligent and moral, being the Intelligent Designer and the Moral Lawgiver. And this God is spiritual and supernatural, since He is beyond the physical and natural world. He can do miracles because He has already done the greatest miracle of all: He has created the world. So the evidence points to the existence of a theistic God—one that is infinite, intelligent, perfect, personal, and supernatural. Again, as Robert Jastrow put it,

The scientist's pursuit of the past ends in the moment of creation. This is an exceedingly strange development, unexpected by all but theologians. They have always accepted the word of the Bible: "In the beginning God created the heavens and the earth."[34]

The conclusion of science about the universe's origin ends where the Bible begins.

---

[34] Jastrow, *God and the Astronomers*, 115.

A Critique of *The Shack*[1]

*T*he Shack is a gripping story about how a person can come to grips with the tragedy of physical evil. Millions have read it and, admittedly, multitudes have been helped in their attempt to overcome the sorrow and grief brought by the death of a loved one. As such, one would be reluctant to give it a negative critique, but ultimately our concern is with truth, not mere comfort. Sometimes error seems more comforting than truth—at least for a time. In any event, our evaluation here of a very popular book is concerned with whether it is a realistic and biblical solution to an age-old problem. (The rest of this appendix is an edited version of the article that appears at *www .normgeisler.com.*)

The Shack: Where Tragedy Confronts Eternity by William P. Young (Newbury Park, CA: Windblown Media, 2007) is a *New York Times* bestseller with well over a million copies in print. While many have been blessed by its message, its message is precisely what calls for scrutiny.

Responses range from eulogy to heresy. On the positive

---

[1] For a more detailed examination of doctrinal deviation in *The Shack*, see James DeYoung's book, *Burning Down 'the Shack'* (WND Books, 2010).

side, Eugene Peterson, author of *The Message*, predicted that it "has the potential to do for our generation what John Bunyan's *Pilgrim's Progress* did for his. It's that good!" Emmy award-winning ABC producer Patrick M. Roddy declares that "it is a one of a kind invitation to journey to the very heart of God. Through my tears and cheers, I have been indeed transformed by the tender mercy with which William Paul Young opened the veil that too often separated me from God and from myself" (*http://theshackbook.com/endorsements.html*). People from all walks of life are raving about the work of the heretofore unknown "Willie" Young, born in Canada, son of a pastor/missionary, and a graduate of Warner Pacific College in Portland, Oregon.

BACKGROUND OF THE BOOK

The Shack is Christian fiction that communicates in a casual, easy-to-read, non-abrasive manner. From his personal experience, Young attempts to answer some of life's biggest questions: Who is God? Who is Jesus? What is the Trinity? What is salvation? Is Jesus the only way to heaven? If God, then why evil? What happens after I die?

In the final section, titled "The Story behind *The Shack*," Young reveals that the motivation for this story comes from his own struggle with difficult issues. He claims his seminary training just didn't provide answers to many of his pressing questions. Then one day in 2005, he felt God whisper in his ear that this was going to be his year of Jubilee and restoration. Out of that experience he felt led to write *The Shack*.

According to Young, much of the book was formed around personal conversations with God, family, and friends (258–259). He says the main character, Mack, is a fictional character used to communicate the book's message. However, he admits his children would "recognize that Mack is mostly me, that Nan is a lot like Kim, that Missy and Kate and the other characters often resemble our family members and friends" (259).

THE BASIC STORY

The story centers on a note that Mack, the husband and father, received from "Papa," supposed to be God the Father. It reads, "Mackenzie, It's been a while. I've missed you. I'll be at the shack next weekend if you want to get together" (19). From this, the tale moves through personal struggles with such questions as: Why would someone send me this letter? Does God really speak through letters? How would my seminary training respond to this interaction between God and man? The account takes a turn when Mack's son almost drowns while canoeing; during the chaos, his daughter is abducted and eventually killed. This is what caused Mack to fall into "The Great Sadness," a time period intended to reflect his spiritual condition after the death of his daughter and the questions he's long been asking.

Mack packs his bags and heads for the shack. The point of this journey is to suggest that his traditional teaching, prayers, Sunday hymns, and approach to Christianity were wrong. He comes to the conclusion that "cloistered spirituality seemed to change nothing in the lives of people he knew, except maybe Nan [his wife]" (63). Through this interaction with God, Young uses this fictional encounter as a vehicle for Mack's spiritual journey.

Mack discovers that God is not what we expect Him to be. God the Father is a "large beaming African-American woman." Jesus appeared to be "Middle Eastern and was dressed like a laborer, complete with tool belt and gloves," and the Holy Spirit is named Sarayu, "a small, distinctively Asian woman." The book identifies these people as the Trinity (80–82). After trying to reconcile his seminary training with this new divine encounter, Mack concludes that what he had learned previously was of no help.

AN EVALUATION OF THE BOOK

Young's point is clear: Forget your preconceived notions about God, forget your formal training, and realize that God chooses to appear to us in whatever form we personally need; He's like a mixed metaphor. We cannot fall back onto our religious conditioning (91). *The Shack* attempts to present a Christian worldview through the genre of religious fiction, but just how Christian it is remains to be seen.

Problem One: A Rejection of Traditional Christianity

Beneath the surface of *The Shack* is a rejection of traditional Christianity (179), which, allegedly, must be revised in order to be understood, reminiscent of Brian McClaren's *Everything Must Change*. However, perhaps we ought to question whether it is *Christianity* that needs revision or *Christians* who need to be revitalized. One thing is certain: Christianity should not be rejected merely because it has some hypocritical representatives. To be sure, some seminary training is bad, and even good seminary training doesn't help if you don't heed it. But we shouldn't throw out the baby with the bathwater. Christ established His church and said the gates of hell would not prevail against it (Matthew 16:16–18). *The Shack,* gripping as its story is, trades a church occupied with people who hear the Word of God preached for an empty shack where there is neither.

Problem Two: Experience Trumps Revelation

An underlying error with *The Shack*'s message is that it uses personal experience to trump revelation. The solutions to life's basic problems come from extra-biblical experience, not from Scripture (80–100). Non-biblical voices are given precedent over the biblical voice of God. These alleged "revelations" from the "Trinity" are the basis of the whole story. While biblical truth is alluded to, it is not the message's authoritative basis. In the final analysis, experience interprets the Bible; it is not the Bible that interprets experience. This leads to a denial of fundamental Protestant teaching.

Problem Three: The Rejection of Sola Scriptura

The Shack rejects Scripture's sole authority to determine matters of faith and practice. Rather than receiving comfort and counsel from God's Word, Mack is instructed to go to an empty shack in the wilderness and get from extra-biblical voices all he needs to cope with life's tragedies.

> In seminary he had been taught that God had completely stopped any overt communication with moderns, preferring to have them only listen to and follow sacred Scripture. . . . God's voice had been reduced to paper. . . . It seemed that direct communication with God was something exclusively for the ancients. . . . Nobody wanted God in a box, just in a book. (63)

However, the Bible clearly declares that "Scripture is God-breathed and is useful for teaching, rebuking, correcting and training in righteousness, so that the man of God may be thoroughly equipped for every good work" (2 Timothy 3:16–17). Our comfort is realized in that through "the encouragement of the Scriptures we might have hope" (Romans 15:4). In short, God's Word is sufficient for faith and practice. No "new truth" is needed for doctrine or living the Christian life.

Of course, this does not mean God cannot bring biblical principles to our minds when needed through various experiences, even tragic ones. He can and He does. Nor does it mean God cannot guide in circumstances that help us in the application of biblical principles to our lives. He can and He does. But these experiences bring no new revelation—they are the occasion for God focusing our attention on the only infallible written source of His revelation, the Bible alone. To forsake this fundamental principle is to leave Protestantism for mysticism.

Problem Four: An Unbiblical View of the Nature and Triunity of God

In addition to an errant view of Scripture, *The Shack* has an unorthodox view of the Trinity. God appears as three separate persons (in three separate bodies), which seems to support tritheism, even though the author denies it ("We are not three gods") along with modalism ("We are not talking about One God with three attitudes" [100]). Nonetheless, Young departs from God's essential nature for a social relationship among the members of the Trinity. He wrongly stresses the plurality of God as three separate persons, and, according to Young, God's unity is not in one essence (nature), as the orthodox view holds. Rather, it is a social union of three separate persons.

In addition to the false teaching that God the Father and

the Holy Spirit have physical bodies (see John 4:24), the members of the Trinity are not *separate* persons; they are *distinct* persons in one divine nature. In the same way, a triangle has three distinct corners yet is one triangle; it does not have three separate corners (it would not be a triangle if its corners were separated from it). God is one in essence and has three distinct (but inseparable) Persons.

Problem Five: An Unbiblical View of Punishing Sin

Another claim is that God does not need to punish sin:

> Papa stopped her preparations and turned toward Mack. He could see a deep sadness in her eyes. "I am not who you think I am, Mackenzie. I don't need to punish people for sin. Sin is its own punishment, devouring you from the inside. It is not my purpose to punish it; it's my joy to cure it" (119).

As welcoming as this message may be, at best it reveals a dangerously imbalanced understanding of God. In addition to being loving and kind, God is also holy and just; because He is just He must punish sin. "The soul who sins will die" (Ezekiel 18:4 NASB); "I am holy," says the Lord (Leviticus 11:44). God is "of purer eyes than to see evil and cannot look at wrong" (Habakkuk 1:13 ESV); "The wages of sin is death" (Romans 6:23); " 'Vengeance is mine, I will repay' says the Lord" (12:19 ESV).

In short, *The Shack* presents a lopsided view of God as love but not justice. This undermines the faith's central message— that Christ died for our sins and rose from the dead (1 Corinthians 15:1-6). Some emergent-church leaders have given an even more frontal and near blasphemous attack on Christ's sacrificial atonement, calling it a "form of cosmic child abuse—a vengeful father, punishing his son for offences he has not even committed" (Steve Chalke, *The Lost Message of Jesus,* 184). Such is the end of the logic that denies an awesomely holy God who cannot tolerate sin was satisfied (propitiated) on behalf of our sin (1 John 2:1). Christ paid the penalty for us "so that in him we might become the righteousness of God" (2 Corinthians 5:21), suffering "the just for the unjust, so that He might bring us to God" (1 Peter 3:18 NASB).

Problem Six: A False View of the Incarnation

Another area of concern is a false view of the person and work of Christ: "When we three spoke ourself into human existence as the Son of God, we became fully human. We also chose to embrace all the limitations that this entailed. Even though we have always been present in this universe, we now became flesh and blood" (98). This is a serious misunderstanding of the Incarnation. The whole Trinity was not incarnated; only the Son was (John 1:14), and in His case *deity did not become humanity.* Rather, the Second Person of the Godhead *assumed a human nature in addition to His divine nature.* Neither the Father nor the Holy Spirit (who are pure spirit—John 4:24) became human.

Problem Seven: A Wrong View of the Way of Salvation

According to Young, Christ is the "best" way to relate to the Father, not the only way (109). The "best" means that there may be other ways to relate to God. Such an assertion is contrary to Jesus' claim, "I am the way and the truth and the life. No one comes to the Father except through me" (John 14:6). He added, "Whoever believes in Him [Christ] is not condemned, but whoever does not believe stands condemned already because he has not believed in the name of God's one and only Son" (3:18). Jesus is not merely the best way; He is the only way to God. "There is one God and one mediator between God and men, the man Christ Jesus" (1 Timothy 2:5).

Problem Eight: A Heretical View of the Father Suffering

The book also contains a classic heresy called patripassianism (lit: Father Suffering). Young claims God the Father suffered along with the Son: " 'Haven't you seen the wounds on Papa [God the Father] too?' I didn't understand them. 'How could he . . . ?' 'For love. He chose the way of the cross . . . because of love' " (165). But both the Apostles' Creed and the Nicene Creed (AD 325) make it very clear that Jesus alone "suffered" for us on the cross. And He did this only through His human nature. To say otherwise is to engage in "confusing the two natures" of Christ, explicitly condemned in the Chalcedonian Creed (AD 451). Suffering is a form of change, and the Bible makes it very clear that God cannot change (Malachi 3:6; James 1:17; Hebrews 1:10–12).

Problem Nine: A Denial of Hierarchy in the Godhead

The Shack also claims there is no hierarchy in God or in human communities modeled after Him. Supposedly, hierarchy exists only as a result of the human struggle for power:

> "I know that there are three of you. But you respond with such graciousness to each other. Isn't one of you more the boss than the other two. . . . I have always thought of God the Father as

sort of being the boss and Jesus as the one following orders, you know, being obedient. . . ."

"Mackenzie, we have no concept of final authority among us; only unity. We are in a circle of relationship, not a chain of command. . . . What you're seeing here is relationship without any overlay of power. . . . Hierarchy would make no sense among us" (121).

Young gives no biblical support for this egalitarian view of God and human relations—and for good reason, since Scripture clearly affirms there *is* an order of authority in the Godhead, the home, and the church. Submission and obedience are biblical terms. Jesus submitted to the Father (Matthew 26:39): "He humbled himself and became obedient to [the point of] death" (Philippians 2:8). In heaven "the Son Himself also will be subjected to the One who subjected all things to Him, so that God may be all in all" (1 Corinthians 15:28 NASB).

Children are to submit to their parents (Ephesians 6:1). Likewise, wives are urged to: "Submit to your husbands as to the Lord" (5:22). "The head of every man is Christ, and the head of the woman is man, and the head of Christ is God" (1 Corinthians 11:3). Members are to "obey your leaders and submit to their authority" (Hebrews 13:17). Citizens are commanded "to be subject to rulers and authorities, to be obedient" (Titus 3:1).

The hierarchical order in the Godhead is the basis for all human relationships. And pure love does not eliminate this; it demands it. "This is the love of God, that we keep His commandments" (1 John 5:3 NASB). Portraying God as a Mother, rather than a Father, reveals an underlying anti-masculinity in Young's thought.

> Males seem to be the cause of so much of the pain in the world.
> They account for most of the crime and many of those are per-
> petrated against women. . . . The world, in many ways, would be
> a much calmer and gentler place if women ruled. There would
> have been far fewer children sacrificed to the gods of greed and
> power. (148)

He does not explain how this would not be a hierarchy if women "ruled" the world.

Problem Ten: Ignoring the Church's Role in Edifying Believers

The Shack is totally silent about the crucial role the community of believers plays for individuals needing encouragement. In fact, there is a kind of anti-church current in reaction
to a hypocritical, legalistic, abusive father who was a church
leader (1–3). This clearly is anti-biblical. A bad church should
not be replaced with no church but with a better church. God
gave the church "pastors and teachers, for the equipping of the
saints . . . to the building up of the body of Christ" (Ephesians
4:11–12 NASB). Paul said, "To each one [in the body] is given
the manifestation of the Spirit for the common good" (1 Corinthians 12:7 NASB).

Young replaces a Bible-based church in the wildwood
with a Bible-less shack in the wild. Comfort in bereavement
is sought in a lonely shack where one is to find comfort by
heeding subjective divine presentations. At this point, several
scriptural exhortations about being aware of deceiving spirits come to mind (1 Timothy 4:1; 1 John 4:1; 2 Corinthians
11:14). As for the need for a church, we are "not [to] give up
meeting together, as some are in the habit of doing, but let us
encourage one another—and all the more as you see the Day

approaching" (Hebrews 10:25). Without the regular meeting with a body of edifying believers, proper Christian growth inevitably is stunted.

Problem Eleven: An Inclusivistic View of Who Will Be Saved

While *The Shack* falls short of the universalism ("All will be saved") found in other emergent writings, it does have a wide-sweeping inclusivism whereby virtually anyone through virtually any religion can be saved apart from Christ.

> Jesus [said] . . . "Those who love me come from every system that exists. They are Buddhists or Mormons, Baptist, or Muslims . . . and many who are not part of any Sunday morning or religious institution. . . . Some are bankers and bookies, Americans and Iraqis, Jews and Palestinians. I have no desire to make them Christians, but I do want to join them in their transformation into sons and daughters of my Papa. . . ."

> "Does that mean . . . that all roads will lead to you?"

> "Not at all. . . . Most roads don't lead anywhere. What it does mean is that I will travel any road to find you" (184).

Again, there is no biblical support for these claims. On the contrary, the Scriptures affirm that there is no salvation apart from knowing Christ (Acts 4:12; 1 Timothy 2:5; John 3:18, 36; 8:24).

Problem Twelve: A Wrong View of Faith and Reason

The Shack embraces an irrational view of faith: "There are times when you choose to believe something that would normally be considered absolutely irrational. It doesn't mean that it is actually irrational, but it is surely not rational" (64). Even common sense informs us that this is no way to live the Christian life. The Bible says, " 'Come now, let us reason together,' says the Lord" (Isaiah 1:18); give "a reason for the hope that is in you" (1 Peter 3:15 ESV); "Paul . . . reasoned with them from the Scriptures" (Acts 17:2 ESV); "These were more noble-minded . . . [because they examined] the Scriptures daily to see whether these things were so" (Acts 17:11 NASB). "Beloved, believe not every spirit, but try [test] the spirits whether they are of God" (1 John 4:1 KJV). Socrates said, "The unexamined life is not worth living," and reasonable Christians would add, "The unexamined faith is not worth having."

Problem Thirteen: Eliminating Knowledge of God

According to Young, God is wholly other; we can't really know Him: "I am God. I am who I am. And unlike you . . ." (96). "I am what some would say 'holy and wholly other than you' " (97). "I am not merely the best version of you that you can think of. I am far more than that; above and beyond all that you can ask or think" (97). This view is self-defeating. How could we know God is "wholly other"? Wholly other than what? And how can we know what God is not unless we know what He is? Totally negative knowledge of God is impossible.

Further, according to the Bible, we can know what God is really like from both general and special revelation. "Since the creation of the world His invisible attributes, His eternal power and divine nature, have been clearly seen" (Romans 1:20 NASB). Jesus said, "If you had known Me, you would have known My Father also" (John 14:7 NASB), and "He who has seen Me, has seen the Father" (v. 9). God does speak of Himself in His written Word (2 Timothy 3:16), and He tells us something about the way He really is. His words are not deceptive but descriptive.

Problem Fourteen: The Entailing of Divine Deception

In *The Shack*, God is revealed in ways contrary to His nature. The Father is revealed as a woman and having a body, when He is neither. The reason given is that in love God revealed Himself in ways that would be acceptable to the recipient (who had a bad father image). But this is a case of divine deception. God is a spirit (John 4:24) and has no body (Luke 24:39). God is never called a mother in the Bible. It is deceptive to portray His nature in any way that He is not, even if one's motive is loving (91–92). A lie told with a loving motive is still untrue.

Of course, when God speaks to finite creatures, He engages in adaptation to human limits, but never in accommodation to human error. Portraying God as having a black female body is like saying storks bring babies. Young calls it a "mask" that falls away (111). But God does not have masks, and He does not masquerade. "It is impossible for God to lie" (Hebrews 6:18; cf. Titus 1:2). It is the devil, the father of lies, who appears in forms that misrepresent Him (2 Corinthians 11:14). To be sure, there are biblical figures of speech—e.g., God as a rock or a hen—but they are known to be metaphorical and not literal (there are no immaterial rocks, and God does not have feathers).

CONCLUSION

The Shack may well engage the current culture, but not without compromising Christian truth. The book may be psychologically helpful to many who read it, but it is doctrinally harmful. It has a false understanding of God, the Trinity, the person and work of Christ, the nature of man, the institution of the family and marriage, and the nature of the gospel. For those not trained in orthodox doctrine, this book is very dangerous. It promises good news for the suffering but undermines the only good news about Christ's suffering for us. In the final analysis, only truth is truly liberating: "You will know the truth, and the truth will set you free" (John 8:32).

The Shack promises to transform people's lives, but it lacks the transforming power of God's Word (Hebrews 4:12) and the community of believers (10:25). In the final analysis, this book, doctrinally speaking, is more of a *Pilgrim's Regress*.

Bibliography

Anselm. *Cur Deus Homo*. Edited and translated by Thomas Williams. Indianapolis: Hackett, 2007.

Augustine. *Anti-Manichaean Writings*. Whitefish, MT: Kessinger, 2005.

———. *City of God*. New York: Penguin, 2003.

———. *Confessions*. New York: Penguin, 1961.

Baldwin, Lindley. *Samuel Morris*. Minneapolis: Bethany House, 1942. Still in print.

Barrow, J. D. *The Anthropic Cosmological Principle*. New York: Oxford University Press, 1988.

Behe, Michael. *Darwin's Black Box*. New York: Free Press, 2006.

———. *The Edge of Evolution*. New York: Free Press, 2008.

Beisner, Calvin. *Man, Economy, and Environment in Biblical Perspective*. Moscow, ID: Canon, 1994.

———. *Prospects for Growth: A Biblical View of Population Resources, and the Future*. Wheaton, IL: Crossway, 1990.

———. *Prosperity and Poverty: The Compassionate Use of Resources in a World of Scarcity*. Wheaton, IL: Crossway, 1988.

Brandewie, Ernest. *Wilheim Schmidt and the Origin of the Idea of God*. Lanham, MD: Rowman & Littlefield, 1983.

Budziszewski, J. "Objections, Obstacles, Acceptance," interview by Ignatius Press. Ft. Collins, CO, 2006.

Camus, Albert. *The Rebel*. New York: Vintage, 1992.

———. *The Plague*. New York: Penguin, 1988.

Collins, Francis. *The Language of God*. New York: Free Press, 2007.

Craig, William Lane. *The Kalam Cosmological Argument*. Eugene, OR: Wipf & Stock, 2000.

Crick, Francis. *Life Itself: Its Origin and Nature*. New York: Simon & Schuster, 1981.

Crockett, W., ed. *Four Views on Hell*. Grand Rapids, MI: Zondervan, 1992.

Davidson, Bruce W. "Reasonable Damnation: How Jonathan Edwards Argued for the Rationality of Hell" in *The Journal of the Evangelical Theological Society* (3/95), Vol. 38, No. 1.

Dawkins, Richard. *The Blind Watchmaker*. London: The Folio Society, 2008.

Dembski, William. *The End of Christianity: Finding a Good God in an Evil World*. Nashville: B&H Academic, 2009.

Eddy, Mary Baker. *Science and Health with Key to the Scriptures*. First Church of Christ, Scientist, 1934.

Edwards, Jonathan. *The Works of Jonathan Edwards*. Carlisle, PA: Banner of Truth Trust, 1979, reprint.

Flannery, Austin. *Vatican Council II*. Grand Rapids, MI: Eerdmans, 1975.

Flew, Antony, with Roy Abraham Varghese. *There Is a God: How the World's Most Notorious Atheist Changed His Mind*. New York: HarperOne, 2008.

Fraser, James George. *The Golden Bough*. General Books LLC, 2010.

Geisler, Norman. *Baker Encyclopedia of Christian Apologetics*. Grand Rapids, MI: Baker Academic, 1999.

———. *Chosen But Free,* 3rd edition. Minneapolis: Bethany House, 2010.

———. *Christian Ethics,* 2nd edition. Grand Rapids, MI: Baker Academic, 1989.

———. "Man's Destiny: Free or Forced" in *Christian Scholar's Review,* Vol. IX, No. 2 , 1979.

Geisler, Norman, and Winfried Corduan. *Philosophy of Religion.* Eugene, OR: Wipf & Stock, 2003.

Geisler, Norman. *The Roots of Evil.* Eugene, OR: Wipf & Stock, 2002.

———. *Systematic Theology,* Vols I–IV. Minneapolis: Bethany House, 2001–2004.

Gerstner, John. *Jonathan Edwards on Heaven and Hell.* Soli Deo Gloria Ministries, 1999.

Gonzalez, Guillermo, and Jay Richards. *The Privileged Planet.* Washington, DC: Regnery Publishing, Inc, 2004.

Heeren, Fred. *Show Me God.* DayStar Productions, 2004.

Hick, John. "Divine Omnipotence and Human Freedom" in *New Essays in Philosophical Theology,* n.d.

Hoyle, Sir Fred, and Chandra Wickramasinghe. *Evolution from Space.* New York: Simon & Schuster, 1984.

Hume, David. *Letters.* BiblioBazaar, 2009.

Jastrow, Robert. *God and the Astronomers.* Readers Library, 2000.

———. Interview in *Christianity Today,* August 6, 1983.

Kushner, Harold. *When Bad Things Happen to Good People.* New York: Anchor, 2004.

Leibniz, Wilhelm Gottfried. *Theodicy.* BiblioBazaar, 2007.

Lewis, C. S. *The Abolition of Man.* New York: HarperOne, 2001.

———. *God in the Dock.* Grand Rapids, MI: Eerdmans, 1970.

———. *The Great Divorce.* New York: Macmillan, 1946.

————. *A Grief Observed*. Elam Publications, 2008.

————. *Mere Christianity*. Granite Publishers, 2006.

————. *The Problem of Pain*. New York: Macmillan, 1940.

————. *The Screwtape Letters*. New York: Macmillan, 1952.

Mbiti, John. *African Religions and Philosophy*. UK: Heinemann, 1992.

Meyer, Stephen. *Signature in the Cell*. New York: HarperOne, 2009.

McMillen, S. I., and David Stern. *None of These Diseases*. Grand Rapids, MI: Revell, 2000.

Mill, John Stuart. *Nature, the Utility of Religion, and Theism*. Adamant Media Corporation, 2000.

Milton, John. *Paradise Lost*. Modern Library, 2008.

Morris, Henry. *Scientific Creationism*. Boulder, CO: New Leaf Press, Master Books, 1985.

Morris, Henry, and John Whitcomb. *The Genesis Flood*. Grand Rapids, MI: Baker, 1979.

Nietzsche, Friedrich. *Toward a Genealogy of Morals* in Walter Kaufmann, *The Portable Nietzsche*. New York: Viking, 1968.

Pascal, Blaise. *Pensees*. Indianapolis: Hackett, 2005.

Pember, G. H. *Earth's Earliest Ages*. Whitefish, MT: Kessinger, 2003.

Plantinga, Alvin. *God, Freedom, and Evil*. Grand Rapids, MI: Eerdmans, 1977.

Ross, Hugh. *The Creator and the Cosmos*. Downers Grove, IL: NavPress, 1995.

Russell, Bertrand. "Why I Am Not a Christian" in *The Writings of Bertrand Russell*. New York: Simon & Schuster, 1961.

Sagan, Carl. *Broca's Brain*. New York: Ballantine, 1993.

————. *Cosmos*. New York: Random, 2002.

Sandage, Allan. Cited in *Truth,* 1985.

Sartre, Jean-Paul. *No Exit and Three Other Plays.* New York: Vantage, 1947.

———. *Words.* New York: Penguin, 2002.

Stoner, Don. *A New Look at an Old Earth.* Eugene, OR: Harvest House, 1997.

Strong, A. H. *Systematic Theology.* n.p., 1889.

Tada, Joni Eareckson. *A Step Further.* Grand Rapids, MI: Zondervan, 1991.

Thomas Aquinas. *Summa Theologica.* Allen, TX: Christian Classics, 1981.

Voltaire. *Candide.* New York: Simon & Schuster, 2005.

Yancey, Philip. *Where Is God When It Hurts?* Grand Rapids, MI: Zondervan, 2002.

Yockey, Herbert. *Journal of Theoretical Biology,* 1981.

Zacharias, Ravi, and Norman Geisler. *Who Made God?* Grand Rapids, MI: Zondervan, 2003.

Norman L. Geisler

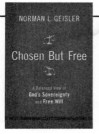

In recent years the controversy between free will and predestination has intensified, leaving many wondering if it even matters. Using biblically sound arguments, Dr. Geisler affirms both the sovereignty and foreknowledge of God and the human responsibility to receive or reject Him—and why this answer is so important to our lives.

Chosen But Free

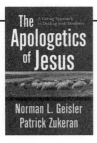

In this hard-hitting resource, you will discover a fresh and practical approach to apologetics—taken directly from the ultimate apologist, Jesus Christ.
"Through this landmark work, you will understand in a new way the genius and power of the arguments Christ made in his teachings and his defense."—Josh D. McDowell, author and speaker

The Apologetics of Jesus (co-written with Patrick Zukeran)

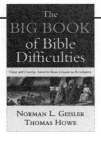

This comprehensive and user-friendly volume offers clear and concise answers to every major Bible difficulty from Genesis to Revelation. Written in a problem/solution format, the book covers over eight hundred questions that critics and doubters raise about the Bible. Three extensive indexes offer quick and easy access to the answers you need.

The Big Book of Bible Difficulties (co-written with Thomas Howe)